ZERO DOWN YOUR DEBT

Reclaim Your Income and Build a Life You'll Love

**HOLLY PORTER JOHNSON
& GREG JOHNSON**

Founders of ClubThrifty.com

"Want to live a life free from financial stress but don't know where to start? *Zero Down Your Debt* provides actionable steps to kill your debt and live the kind of life you want - all through one simple tool, a budget. Holly and Greg are perfect examples of how to do it and how you can live with financial confidence."

- John Schmoll, Personal Finance Expert and Founder of Frugal Rules

"Holly and Greg provide the kind of no nonsense guidance that anyone struggling with their finances needs to hear. Get unstuck with the strategies and solutions this powerhouse duo used to rid themselves of their own financial struggle and create financial (and lifestyle) freedom."

- Stefanie O'Connell, Millennial Money Expert

"*Zero Down Your Debt* is a wake-up call for everyone who thinks they can't live the life they want because they're struggling with debt. Holly and Greg are living proof that it can be done – not by winning the lottery or striking it rich but by budgeting."

- Cameron Huddleston, Award-Winning Personal Finance Journalist

"I've been a fan of Holly and Greg's work for years, and they provide actionable and real-life advice that applies to my life in multiple ways. I'm excited that their book is out and I know that it will help millions of families out there take hold of their finances. Personal finance isn't always fun but Holly and Greg have great personalities that come out in their writing and make reading more enjoyable!"

-Harry Campbell, Founder & Owner of The Rideshare Guy

"A budget isn't a bad thing – it's your ticket to the debt-free life and, maybe, your ticket into a lifestyle that YOU choose. That's how Holly Porter Johnson and her husband were able to pay off $50,000 worth of debt, leave jobs that were physically and emotionally exhausting, and create a new life: self-employed, debt-free and able to spend more time with their children.

Not everyone wants to be his own boss, but how many people would give anything just to be able to control their cash? Whether you're living paycheck to paycheck or merely wondering where your money goes each month, "*Zero Down Your Debt*" provides a step-by-step plan on taking back the reins.

What indebted people DON'T need is an ivory-tower economist wagging a judgmental finger. What they DO need is someone like Johnson, who writes from a place of understanding. She uses their own experience (working brutally long hours, overspending, running up debts, not saving for emergencies) to illustrate how she and her husband changed their money habits and, ultimately, their lives.

If you've always been afraid of budgets, *Zero Down Your Debt* will give you a new way of looking at money management. As the author says, "A zero-sum budget is the key to getting what you want out of life." Quite literally, the book gives consumers the tools to change their lives."

- Donna Freedman, Personal Finance Writer and Author of *Your Playbook for Tough Times: Living Large On Small Change, For The Short Term Or Long Haul*

"Holly and Greg Johnson's *Zero Down Your Debt* is a must read for anyone and everyone who has ever had debt. This great read will help you manage a better budget, get your money in order, and whip you into financial shape. Debt can be a big obstacle in life, but by reading *Zero Down Your Debt*, you'll be able to destroy your debt in no time."

- Michelle Schroeder-Gardner, Award-Winning Personal Finance Expert and Writer at MakingSenceofCents.com

"Debt freedom is not a myth from which fairy tales are made of. Debt Freedom is not an out of reach goal that can only be obtained by a select group of special and unique individuals. Debt freedom is a very real and a very attainable objective that you have the ability to reach.

Zero Down Your Debt is the definitive resource that will help you do just that. Greg and Holly share their heart and their personal journey to debt freedom in a very practical way that will propel you forward and allow you to achieve debt freedom in your own life. Anyone who commits to following the advice outlined in these pages will revolutionize their financial situation for the better, and allow the stresses that come along with being buried in debt to begin to fade away."

- Talaat and Tai McNeely, Personal Finance Educators and Founders of HisandHerMoney.com

"Greg and Holly Johnson are experts when it comes to getting out of debt and creating the right mindset to manage your money. This book is a must read for millennial families looking to budget in the 21st century."

- Robert Farrington, Founder of The College Investor

"*Zero Down Your Debt* is real world and something you can implement right away! Holly and Greg don't teach from theory, but rather from their own experiences with managing money, life, and everything in between. Instead of wondering where you will end up, this book will show you how to get there."

- Chris Peach, Founder of the Award-Winning Blog, Money Peach

"*Zero Down Your Debt* covers the Johnson's inspirational journey to paying off over $50,000 of debt. But the most impactful words are sprinkled throughout the book in the action items. A good book inspires you to take action but this book gives you the answer to "how do I take action?" Holly and Greg have truly figured out the key to financial success and created a transformational read."

- LaTisha Styles, Finance Expert

"Holly and Greg have written a manifesto for debt abolishers everywhere. Are you ready to change your life today? Devote a few hours now to the easy steps in this book and the rest of your life to financial freedom. I can't imagine a better rate of return on your time!"

- Joe Saul-Sehy, Host of the Award-Winning Stacking Benjamins Podcast

For permission requests, please contact the publisher at:

Mango Publishing Group

2850 Douglas Road, 3rd Floor

Coral Gables, FL 33134 USA

info@mango.bz

For special orders, quantity sales, course adoptions and corporate sales, please email the publisher at sales@mango.bz.

For trade and wholesale sales, please contact Ingram Publisher Services at customer.service@ingramcontent.com or +1.800.509.4887.

ZERO DOWN YOUR DEBT: Reclaim Your Income and Build a Life You'll Love

ISBN: 978-1-63353-479-7

Printed in the United States of America

Table of Contents

Just a decade ago, I spent most of my waking hours in a stressful, thankless job that made me miserable. Chronic back pain didn't help, either. After two spinal fusions in my early 20s and complications after my first pregnancy, the constant ache consumed both my energy and my life force, making common tasks and even living and breathing a chore.

When you're in pain, everything simply seems a whole lot worse. Working 40 to 50 hours a week with young children, a house, and all that jazz is hard enough if you're healthy. But imagine doing it all with a knife in your back; that's exactly how I felt.

Yet, I endured it. What choice did I have? We were earning a nice income but absolutely broke in terms of real wealth. We were going through the motions and bringing in steady paychecks, but simultaneously getting nowhere. We were spending every dollar we earned and then some, making it impossible for me to take a lower-paying job, reduce my hours, or try something new. Simply put, we were stuck – or at least I was.

In a lot of ways, my husband had it even worse. He worked in the mortuary business for over a decade, and I was by his side for seven of those years. While I slaved away working crazy hours as our admin and senior event coordinator, my husband's hours were more like 24/7, 365. Yep, as a mortician, he was on call constantly. So, when the phone would ring – at any time of the day or night – he would have to rush out.

And his hours were brutally inconsistent. Ask anyone in the funeral industry and they'll tell you it's either extremely busy or not busy at all. Most of the time, you're either working a million hours or busy playing Candy Crush Soda Saga.

Sure, funeral home customers are stressed out by the time they get to the mortuary, but there was something comforting about being their rock. For many years, it was enough to dull my back pain and justify the long hours my husband put in. Even when we were feeling down in the dumps or helpless, we could name 10 people who were having the absolute worst day of their lives. That helped us keep things in perspective.

Over the years, we heard and saw it all. From families squabbling over money to sad stories of those who died much too soon, we experienced a merry-go-round of teachable and life-changing moments that made us reflect on the way we ourselves were living. We buried people who retired and dropped dead the next day, young parents who were taken in freak auto accidents, and 30-year-olds with terminal cancer. We saw babies hug their dead fathers for the last time and parents drop to their knees at the sight of their departed children. We listened to them cry, and sometimes we cried with them.

At a certain point, though, we'd had enough. As I mentioned, I was schlepping to work with chronic pain that coupled with constant, utter sadness. And even though my husband, Greg, fared better physically, he had become increasingly frustrated with his long hours and overly demanding schedule.

But we didn't have much more than a dollar to our names. Eventually, the reality of our situation hit us.

As the months passed, and the tragic, unforgettable moments piled up, we started to wonder, "Should we be doing things differently?"

We spent our days listening to people's stories, including their biggest regrets. We woke in the middle of the night to cries and shrieks as people came to terms with what they had lost. We had spent early mornings, late nights, holidays, and weekends sharing people's sorrows – but were we really listening?

> *"What if we died today?" we began to wonder. Would we be happy with what we accomplished? With how we were living?*

Eventually, we started to. And the cosmic shift that took place was nothing short of life-changing. Instead of seeing our customers and thinking to ourselves, "We're so glad it's not us," we began asking a different question: "What if it were?"

"What if we died today?" we began to wonder. Would we be happy with what we accomplished? With how we were living?

Would we be proud? Would we look back and think we had done some amazing things? Would we have no regrets? Was there nothing we would change?

Once we started thinking in these terms, we realized our lives were nothing close to what we wanted them to be. We had no money saved, and thus we had no freedom. We had jobs, but we merely tolerated them. We had debt that weighed us down, yet we weren't doing anything about it. Simply put, we were neglecting ourselves and our dreams.

Working in the funeral industry meant watching people die every day; it meant being painfully aware of our own mortality. We watched as people lived out their worst nightmares, unable to do anything but help them plan their final goodbye.

One would think that if we learned anything from the experience, it might be that nothing matters. We're all gonna die, right? So, what's the point in doing things differently, or changing our lives in uncomfortable ways? What's the point of trying something new or taking a risk? If the end result is always death, what does any of it matter?

Crazy enough, that's not what we learned at all. Instead, we learned that *everything matters*.

We saw how small amounts of money saved over time could lead to real wealth, and that people with modest means but careful plans could live amazing, adventure-filled lives. We learned that young people without a plan grow to be regretful, fearful senior citizens. And we learned that how you treat your parents, how you take care of your body, and how you take care of your money will all matter one day – even if that day seems far, far away.

Most of all, we learned that we wanted our lives to be different – we wanted something more, something amazing. While we were still here on Earth, we wanted to LIVE.

> *"If you wait too long to create the life you want, it will eventually be too late."*

Once we realized we were wasting some of our best years being miserable, we started thinking about what we really wanted.
For me, it was to find a way to leave my job without taking a pay cut and harming my family. I loved working at the mortuary, I really did, but the pain had become unbearable. And at the end of the day, I knew I needed a way out.

But that's not all I wanted. Even though my children were just babies, I wanted to pay for their college educations. I wanted to retire early, travel the world, and experience places and things other people only dream of.

My husband's goals were similar: He wanted a career with better hours, the ability to earn more money, a home that was paid off, and more control over our spending. For him, that also meant getting out of debt as soon as humanly possible. Once we made the commitment, we were ready to put it all behind us and move on... and that's exactly what we did.

Here's the truth no one wants to hear: Inside every elderly man or woman is a young person wondering what the hell happened. In the blink of an eye, you go from 25 to 40 to 60 to 79, and boy, what a ride. But once you reach old age, the dreams you had – or thought you had – begin to die. When you're 82 years old, it's too late to start saving for retirement. With each passing year, the possibilities dwindle. If you wait too long to create the life you want, it will eventually be too late.

Our initial steps were to examine our lives and ask ourselves the big questions: Are we where we want to be? If not, how can we get there? What do we really, truly want out of our lives? If we died today, what would we regret? And what can we do to begin changing that right now?

I wish I could say our journey was easy – that paying off $50,000 in debt, starting a lucrative side business, and changing the way we thought about money was a breeze – but I'd be lying if I did. The truth is, figuring out that we needed to change was a piece of cake. Actually changing ourselves and our behavior? That was an enormous challenge.

We wanted it so badly that we were willing to do *anything* to change our situation for the better. We wanted a new life – one without the pain and stress we had endured for so long – filled with more joy, more fun, and (most of all) more freedom.

The money connection made more and more sense as we plotted our path toward a debt-free, more exciting, and easier life. If we could just get our money straight, we figured, we could live the life we wanted. Unlike some of our customers who had spent decades in careers they hated to retire in a heap of misery and disgust, we could save our money, invest wisely, become more responsible spenders, and create any life of our choosing.

What a gift that realization was! Once we made that connection, we began to see our customers as our potential future selves. We looked at their sometimes tragic ends not just through the lens of shared humanity, but as if we could see ourselves in their shoes.

We began tying their final outcomes to the things they did and didn't do along the way. The father who didn't have life insurance and left a wife and three kids with almost nothing. The couple who saved 10 years for a Hawaiian cruise to celebrate the husband's 55th birthday, only for him to die a week before. And the woman who confessed privately that she'd been counting down to her husband's death for years so she could finally spend all the money she'd saved without guilt.

But for every lesson in what not to do, we also found stories of inspiration. We buried people who lived full, wonderful lives without an ounce of regret (according to their loved ones, anyway), and we saw ends that were both dignified and motivating. We buried people who were true heroes – beloved by their families, accomplished, and seemingly at peace with everything left done and undone. And we knew that's what we wanted.

By now you're probably wondering what all of this has to do with you. But just as we were inspired to change our lives, there's a reason you picked up this book, too. Perhaps the title spoke to you – the idea of becoming debt-free and accomplishing a list of goals yourself. Or maybe you're just tired of living paycheck to paycheck, and ready for something better – something more.

Either way, **a zero-sum budget is the key to getting what you want out of life**. We suggest "zeroing down your debt" because that is exactly what we did. Can you imagine becoming debt-free without hitting the lottery or receiving a big inheritance? It's time to start.

I believe you can do it with every fiber of my being, and it's not just because I'm an optimist; it's because I've done it myself. With just a paper and pen, my family went from struggling to get by to saving a large percentage of our income, reaching small and mid-sized goals, and planning a future that includes checking off our bucket list – one big goal at a time.

> *"We all have one life to live on this planet – one life! Yet, far too many of us don't really know what we want – just that we don't have it. We spend too much, don't save enough, and believe the lie that it's all out of our hands."*

The amazing part about what I'm suggesting is that you don't even need anything to get started. Other than this book, all you need is a pen, some paper, and a sincere desire to change your life in powerful, long-lasting ways. There's nothing to buy and nothing to download. Yet, following the advice in this book will buy you more freedom than you ever dreamed.

My time in the mortuary business fundamentally changed me, and I feel compelled to share the lessons in this book with everyone who will listen. I feel it's my calling to shake some sense into people before it's too late. We all have one life to live on this planet – one life! Yet, far too many of us don't really know what we want – just that we don't have it. We spend too much, don't save enough, and believe the lie that it's all out of our hands.

It doesn't have to be that way. With the right attitude, anyone can turn their situation around and start living the life they dreamed. Yes, you read that right. Anyone.

An elderly woman once told me that I would look back one day and realize all that mattered was memories. And time is the most important thing, she said – more important than the world's most valuable possessions. "Be careful with your time," she said, because one day you'll look back and realize that "it's the only thing you really ever had."

Hearing those words changed me because I knew they were true. The stuff we buy will all be worthless one day, and the material possessions we pined over won't mean a thing. But how we spent our time – and what kind of lives we lived – will linger in our memories for as long as we have them.

If you're like I was, you're finally realizing you want more than the memories of slaving away at a thankless job, of stressing over your debts, of putting in overtime at work to catch up instead of spending that time with your family. You want more than a mediocre existence; you don't want to look back with regret; you want to look back in awe.

All of that and more can be yours, but you have to truly want it.

Remember, everything matters – even what you're doing right now. And there's no better way to spend your time than plotting your journey out of debt and toward the life of your dreams.

So let's get started.

HOW TO USE THIS BOOK

The purpose of this book is to help you zero down your debt so that you can live a fulfilling and exciting life. That's hard to do when you're constantly working to pay off debt. We want to help you reclaim your power, to put you back in control of your life, and to provide you with options you didn't even know existed.

Sound too good to be true? That's OK. At this point, all we're asking you to do is read the book and apply the system. The rest will take care of itself.

If you do the work, the results *will* come.

ACTION ITEMS

When we think in terms of the big picture, things often feel overwhelming. Getting out of debt can seem the same way. But when we break things down into small, actionable items, large ideas suddenly become manageable. Big goals are always accomplished through a series of small actions, and that is exactly what we are going to do here.

At the beginning of each chapter, we'll provide an overview of what you should learn. Once you've read through the chapter, you'll notice a list of "Action Items" to accomplish. These are simple, small, actionable tasks that you can use to seize control of your finances – one small step at a time. We'll explain exactly what's required, but it's up to you to take it from there and put it into practice.

Just as reading a magazine about weight lifting won't whip you into shape, reading this book without taking action won't get you out of debt. Use the action items like you would a workout routine. Complete the workout, and you'll see the results. Do nothing, and you'll be left making excuses as to why it doesn't work.

THE 10 FUNDAMENTAL TRUTHS OF DESTROYING DEBT AND BUILDING REAL WEALTH

Let's start things off with a bang! Throughout this book, we'll be referring to 10 important principles we believe are the foundations to destroying debt and building real wealth. We think these principles can fundamentally alter the way you think about – and use – the money you earn. In short, if you want to get out of debt and build real wealth, it's absolutely necessary to understand the following 10 keys beliefs.

Truth #1:

Debt is the single biggest obstacle standing between you and the life of your dreams.

When you're in debt, it's hard to save for a vacation, your children's college education, or other financial goals you might have. By and large, debt stands in the way of the things you really want in life, sucking your paycheck into its depths one dollar at a time.

Truth #2:

Your paycheck is your most powerful wealth building tool.

We spend our whole lives hoping to hit the lottery or wishing we could just get a bigger raise at work. But if you learn to harness the power of the money you already earn, you might be surprised by how far you can stretch it. Plenty of people have grown rich with modest incomes and careful planning; you can be one of them.

Truth #3:

Debt is the enemy of income.

Remember how debt sucks away your income one dollar at a time? When you have tons of debts to pay and bills to take care of every month, your income never seems like enough. But when you're debt-free, your income belongs to you, not your debt.

Truth #4:

He who has the gold makes the rules.

Borrowing money gives away your power to others. When you owe money to someone, you're beholden to them and must keep working in service of that debt – not your own goals.

Truth #5:

When you tell your money what to do, it listens. When you don't, it disappears.

When you don't track your spending or live within a budget, any extra money you earn has a way of disappearing – and quickly. But when you tell your money what to do each month, it works magic for your finances.

Truth #6:

A zero-sum budget is the most effective tool for harnessing the power of your paycheck.

Because a zero-sum budget empowers every dollar you earn to pay down debt, start saving, and get ahead with your finances, we believe it's the most effective tool for getting your money straight. And if you aren't zeroing down your debt, you're not doing the best you can.

Truth #7:

Debt neither discriminates nor is cured by income. Rather, it is caused and controlled by spending.

Plenty of rich people are deeply in debt, while many with modest incomes live rich, debt-free lives. That's because debt does not discriminate based on how much you earn. Anyone at any level can dig their way into debt, and anyone willing to rein in their spending can dig their way out.

Truth #8:

Living below your means is the most efficient way to unleash your paycheck's potential.

Living below your means is the best and *only* way to destroy debt and start saving for the future. Spending every dollar you make means you're standing still at best, unable to make progress toward your goals. Spending more than you make is a recipe for financial disaster.

Truth #9:

If you can't pay cash, you can't afford it.

We're brought up to believe that we can, and should, borrow money to buy anything we want. From new furniture to a new wardrobe, using debt to "buy now and pay later" is commonplace. But, our penchant for debt has proved disastrous for our finances. To avoid a life of debt and ongoing bills, it's essential to buy only what you can pay for with cash.

Truth #10:

Your spending decisions have consequences and are a reflection of what you value.

It's easy to think that none of your decisions matter too much. Your monthly cable bill, the daily stop at your favorite coffee shop, and the new car you bring home every few years are no big deal, right? Wrong. Here's the truth: Nearly everything you do with your money matters. Big and small, the decisions you make – *and the decisions you don't make* – will eventually make or break your finances. It's just a matter of time.

> *"Every small action matters. Complete each individual task and you WILL see results."*

WHAT TO EXPECT

There's nothing too complex about what we're suggesting here. The steps are simple and easy to understand. But make no mistake, putting them into practice (and sticking with it) can be incredibly hard. In fact, it could be the hardest "easy" thing you'll ever do.

Some of the steps you'll take may be emotional for you. They may test your patience and resolve. They'll push you to make changes in your life, changes that may feel uncomfortable at first.

It's OK. These feelings are natural. You're human.

But, don't quit. Keep going. Just keep chipping away, one small step at a time. These are the changes that will make a difference in your financial and personal life. This is where it happens. This is where you take control.

Hundreds of thousands of people have done it, and you will too.

So, let's get excited! Let's get pumped up! Let's crush this freakin' debt and start living life on our own terms!!!

Every small action matters. Complete each individual task and you WILL see results.

The journey of 5,000 miles starts with a single step, so let's get stepping!

NOTES

_____

_____

_____

_____

_____

_____

_____

_____

_____

_____

_____

_____

NOTES

_____

_____

_____

_____

_____

_____

_____

_____

_____

_____

NOTES

_____

_____

_____

_____

_____

_____

_____

_____

_____

_____

_____

In this chapter you'll learn:

- Why destroying your debt is the key to building wealth

- How destroying debt has affected our lives

- The 'Golden Rule' of personal finance

- How to assess the damage and acknowledge the problem

DEBT SUCKS.

But you already know that, don't you?

Maybe you're buried in debt and struggling just to keep the bill collectors at bay. Perhaps you're making a good salary but still feel like you're living paycheck to paycheck, unable to save any of the money you have coming in. Or, maybe you're tired of schlepping away at your job and dream of doing more – if only your debt obligations weren't keeping you stuck without any options.

Once you discover how debt is destroying the power of your paycheck and commit to eliminating its burden, you'll be able to live life on your own terms and explore options you never knew existed. You'll be able to harness the power of your paycheck to fund your savings goals *and* spend your money on the things you *really* want.

Pretty cool right?

We think so.

WHAT'S WRONG WITH DEBT?

So, what's wrong with debt anyway? Being in debt is normal, right? Isn't it just a fact of life?

It doesn't have to be.

Yes, debt seems normal in America... almost inevitable. After all, as of 2015, the average indebted American household owes almost $16,000 in credit card debt, over $27,000 in auto loans, and over $48,000 in student loans. And that doesn't even touch mortgage debt! According to the numbers, Americans fork over an average of nearly $6,700 a year in interest payments alone! That's a whopping 9% of the average household income.

That means we're putting more of our income toward interest each year than toward our own retirement savings! When you really think about it, that's absurd. With those figures, it's no wonder so many Americans struggle to make financial progress[1].

While being in debt may seem "normal," we barely comprehend what debt actually means for our lives. We're so used to it hanging around our necks, we've grown numb to its effects. We don't have the foggiest idea what it's costing us.

At least, my husband and I sure didn't... until we finally dug into our debt.

OUR BATTLE WITH DEBT

TRUTH #1:

Debt is the single biggest obstacle standing between you and the life of your dreams.

How do we know? Because we lived it.

For years, we muddled through a normal debt-filled existence. We had a house (with a mortgage), two cars (with car payments), and regular jobs (with student loans). To top it off, our spending was out of control.

Like most people, we never really noticed our debt. We were making a nice living, but we couldn't seem to save a thing... nor did we really care. At the end of the month, we paid our bills but never stuck a dime into our savings accounts.

We had gotten comfortable with our debt. Paying it off was just another part of everyday life. It was there and we knew it, but we didn't grasp what it was costing us.

About that time, going to work became a chore. Jobs we once enjoyed were suddenly becoming more and more of a drag. And, why wouldn't they? We weren't working so we could live the lives we wanted. Instead, we were working simply to pay back our debt.

We had to make a change. Our time in the funeral industry taught us that life is precious. We were giving up our precious time – our lives – to earn money that belonged to our debts, not to us. In essence, we weren't just wasting our money; we were wasting our lives.

So, we pored over our bills, totaled up our debts, and examined our spending habits. We recognized we had a problem. After adding it all up, our total debt (minus the house) was came in around $50,000. We made the immediate decision to pay it off and never go into debt *ever* again.

Over a period of 18 months, we cut back on our spending, used the extra money to aggressively pay down our debts, and ended up destroying every debt we owed but our mortgage.

Finally, we could breathe a small sigh of relief. Our debt was gone, and we felt like we'd hit the lottery. Instead of shelling out thousands of dollars a month toward our debt, we were able to save that money and do with it whatever we pleased.

THE POWER OF YOUR PAYCHECK

Want to know the biggest key to getting out of debt and building wealth? Chances are, you have everything you need – you simply don't know it yet. That's right: Your most powerful wealth building tool is your own paycheck.

It seems obvious, right? But it's absolutely true. The key to growing wealth is earning money. And for the vast majority of us, that means earning a paycheck.

TRUTH #2:

Your paycheck is your most powerful wealth building tool.

Unfortunately, too many of us are quick to dismiss how powerful our paycheck actually is. We think we don't earn enough, and we convince ourselves that we need to earn more money if we ever hope to get ahead. But the vast majority of the time, nothing could be farther from the truth.

In reality, we simply haven't figured out how to harness our paycheck's power...yet. Instead of using our income in service of our own true goals, we buy things we don't need or even want.

Worse, we finance these purchases with money we don't have, undermining the power of our paycheck by shackling it to the service of those debts. Here's another truth that took us a while to grasp:

TRUTH #3: Debt is the enemy of income.

Racking up consumer debt is the fastest way to destroy your income and the ability to build wealth that comes with it. But it's not just the debt itself that hurts. It's the fact that you don't realize how much your debt is really costing you.

When you use debt to finance a purchase, the true cost of what you're buying never sinks in. You put off the pain of purchasing until later. And, when you do it over and over and over again – financing everything from cars to education to furniture – all those monthly payments add up and chip away at your ability to save. Chip, chip, chip. Month after month after month. After a while, instead of working to live, you're working just to pay back debt.

> *"Racking up consumer debt is the fastest way to destroy your income and the ability to build wealth that comes with it. But it's not just the debt itself that hurts. It's the fact that you don't realize how much your debt is really costing you."*

There's nothing fun about schlepping away 40 hours a week so you can turn around and hand over your money to somebody else. But, when that money is yours to keep, everything becomes a lot more exciting.

Instead of getting your paycheck and thinking about all the things you **need** to pay with it, you start dreaming about all the things you **can** do with the money. Rather than thinking, "Well, this needs to go toward the car payment," your thoughts change to, "I'm going to use this money for a trip to Mexico." You stop seeing life as a series of "must-dos" and start looking at all the possibilities life presents.

It's an incredibly freeing feeling, and it's one you can experience by following the ideas in this book.

By protecting your paycheck, you protect your life.

USING THE GOLDEN RULE TO BUILD REAL WEALTH

Perhaps you've heard this one before. It's called the "Golden Rule"... but it might not be the rule you're thinking about. Here's how it goes:

TRUTH #4: He who has the gold makes the rules.

Growing up in your parents' house meant you had to follow their rules. Since your employer controls your paycheck, you have to play by their rules. When you owe money to a lender, you guessed it, the lender makes the rules.

Think about this for a minute: Right now, you're trading your time – your life – to make money. But, when you're in debt, part of every paycheck you bring home literally belongs to somebody else. Every. Single. Month. That means you're giving up part of your life to somebody else. You're not just trading your life for money, you're trading your life for debt. You owe, so you give up control.

That's not all. Borrowing money isn't free. Lenders don't just loan you money out of the kindness of their hearts. You're not just using your life to pay back the sticker price of those items you financed – you're using it to pay interest, too. Debt costs you more and more, often without you even realizing it, killing you softly with each monthly payment.

When you're debt-free, *you* get to choose how you spend your paycheck. *You* have the ability to take risks and live life on your own terms. *You* are in control of your money and your life.

Get out of debt. Make your own rules. Become "the man with the gold."

9 SPECIFIC REASONS DEBT SUCKS

Greg and I have grown to hate debt so much that we could list thousands of reasons you should avoid it like the plague.

Here are some of the most important.

- **Debt is the enemy of income.** Your paycheck is the most important wealth building tool you have. When you're forced to pay off debt each month, part of your income – sometimes even *most* of it – is already spoken for. Debt hacks your paycheck to pieces, and with it your ability to build wealth.

- **Debt makes it hard to get ahead.** Debt effectively decreases your income, making it that much harder to make financial progress. When you're shelling out thousands of dollars to creditors each month, it's pretty freakin' tough to look past tomorrow's bills. And when you're living paycheck to paycheck, things like saving for retirement, college, or even a vacation get put on the back burner.

- **Debt decreases your options.** When you have bills to pay and mouths to feed, big financial risks – like quitting your job to start your dream business – don't look too attractive. And the more bills you have, the less likely you'll be able to take some risks in life. Debt forces you to become a wage slave and destroys your ability to make decisions for yourself. This voluntary purge of your freedom comes at a cost – mentally, emotionally, and monetarily.

- **Debt stresses you out.** Being in debt is downright stressful, especially when you fall behind. Is it any wonder that so many of us walk around depressed, stressed, and angry? Even if you don't have debt collectors harassing you, all that debt hanging around your neck is enough to make you want to crawl into a hole and hide.

- **Debt makes you give up control**. He who has the gold makes the rules. When you owe somebody else, you have to play by their rules. They are in control, not you.

- **Debt forces you to work longer and harder.** Got a giant car payment to worry about? How about a mortgage to pay? When you're in debt, you have to keep feeding the beast – and you're paying more than the sticker price in the form of interest. That means working harder and longer just so you can turn around and give your money to somebody else. Doesn't sound like much fun, does it?

- **Debt hides the true cost.** Debt is a sneaky little devil. It weasels its way in, delaying the pain of a purchase until later. It masks itself, so you don't even realize the true cost of what you've just bought. Accruing more and more debt starts to feel normal... until you can't even distinguish the damage it's doing to your money, your life, and your dreams.

- **Debt is a cycle that keeps building on itself.** Debt never gets better. It only gets worse. The free money is addictive, but it's only hiding the financial pain. The more you use it, the more you need, and the worse it gets. The only way out of it, the only way to heal your finances, is to pay it off.

- **Debt makes everything more expensive.** You didn't think all this "free money" was actually free, did you? Lenders are in the business of making money, and they do it by charging you interest, month after month. Whenever you finance a purchase, you're going to pay more for it in the long run – sometimes *a lot* more.

WHAT CAN YOU DO NOW?

That's all fine and good, you think, and maybe you wish you'd realized it sooner. But, you're *already* in debt – so what should you do now?

We've come to the first step in our journey to debt freedom: **We need to recognize that we have a problem.**

Yes, we are addicted to debt.

We know it's hard to admit, but it's the truth... and it's the first step to recovery.

To really drive home this point, we need to assess the situation, understand the damage we're dealing with, and fully acknowledge the problem. Here's how.

First, bust out all of your bills and stack them into a pile. Now, take out the bills for your monthly living expenses – such as electric and gas utilities, insurance, childcare, cable, internet, and phone bills – and set them aside.

You should now have a pile of bills for items you financed. These might include credit card bills, your mortgage, car payments, furniture financing or store credit card bills, student loans, and other debts. Add up the total balance owed on each bill – not the minimum monthly payment, but the outstanding balance or remaining principal on each loan. This is the total amount of debt you owe. Grab a sheet of paper and write it down.

Next, subtract the amount of mortgage debt you owe from the total. This is your **non-mortgage debt**, and that is what we want you to focus on zeroing down in this book.

Grab another sheet of paper, and this time write down your total non-mortgage debt in the biggest, boldest, most horrifically disgusting gigantic black numbers that will fit on the page.

Look at that monster and see it clearly for what it is. Stare at it and let it sink in.

Shocking, isn't it?

That's your debt... and it is holding you back from the life you deserve.

Keep staring at it until you've *really* internalized what this debt means to you. Understand what this number represents, what that money could have been used for, and how it continues to hold you back.

Let it sink in.

Now, take that piece of paper and destroy it. Crumple it up, light it on fire, or tear that mothereffer to shreds! Scream out to the world and promise yourself, "Never again!"

Your debt doesn't own you, it doesn't define you, and you will overcome it!

When you perform this crazy stunt, you're going to feel a sense of relief, a sense of accomplishment, and a sense of control that you never even knew existed.

Now you know what the problem is. You know what it looks like. It's time to zero it down. It's time to attack.

ACTION ITEMS

Gather all of your debts together. Total them up so you know how much you owe in both total debt and non-mortgage debt. Write it down and internalize it. Acknowledge the problem and understand what it is costing you. Then, reassert your commitment to defeating it.

Don't get intimidated or discouraged. Remember, even the longest journeys start with a single step. We're going to defeat this monster together, one step at a time. You got this.

1. 2015 American Household Credit Card Debt Survey, Nerdwallet, https://www.nerdwallet.com/blog/credit-card-data/average-credit-card-debt-household/, April 15, 2016.

NOTES

_____

_____

_____

_____

_____

_____

_____

_____

_____

_____

_____

NOTES

_____

_____

_____

_____

_____

_____

_____

_____

_____

_____

_____

_____

NOTES

NOTES

_____

_____

_____

_____

_____

_____

_____

_____

_____

_____

_____

In this chapter you'll learn:

- Why making a monthly budget is the most important financial skill you can learn

- How a monthly budget actually creates freedom rather than restrictions

- Why your past budgets have failed

- How to create a monthly budget that actually works

- How to create a budget if you have a variable income

> *"A budget helps us curb these problems. Instead of spending unconsciously, a budget encourages us to spend our money deliberately and with purpose on the things we value most. It stops our paycheck from performing a vanishing act, and protects the money we've worked so hard to earn."*

Ah, budgeting. The dreaded B-word. It just sent shivers down your spine, didn't it?

Seriously, it's OK. There's nothing to be afraid of.

You might not realize it yet, but a budget isn't some steel cage holding you back from the things you want. In fact, it's exactly the opposite.

A budget is a financial tool that, when used properly, can help set you free: Free from the stress of living paycheck to paycheck. Free from the wage-slave mentality that crushes your soul and forces you to stay in a job you despise. Free from the attitude that you'll *never* live life on your own terms and have the experiences you desperately desire.

A budget is your ticket to financial freedom. Let us explain.

TRUTH #5:

When you tell your money what to do, it listens. When you don't, it disappears.

You already know that your paycheck is your most powerful wealth-building tool. Still, most of us squander its potency. Month after month, we buy things without thinking about it. We make purchases here and there, large and small, with no idea how much we're really spending. In short, we waste our paycheck on fake "needs" and impulse buys that don't do anything to fulfill our deeper desires.

We spend without purpose, and – when our paycheck disappears – we have no idea where it went.

A budget helps us curb these problems. Instead of spending unconsciously, a budget encourages us to spend our money deliberately and with purpose on the things we value most. It stops our paycheck from performing a vanishing act, and protects the money we've worked so hard to earn.

Even better, a written budget (yes, we said written) helps us remember how and when we need to put our paycheck to use. It's easy to forget which bills are coming in and when they're due. This can easily trip us up, causing a shortfall for the month. When we're short on cash, it's tempting to use debt to paper over the problem. By using a written budget, however, we'll have a clearly defined, organized plan that helps us get the most out of what we earn.

Harnessing the power of your paycheck is essential for getting out of debt and building wealth. To zero down your debt, you've got to take advantage of *every* last penny at your disposal. A zero-sum budget is your ticket to doing just that.

TRUTH #6:

A zero-sum budget is the most effective tool for harnessing the power of your paycheck.

Knowing how to create a budget is the most important money skill you can learn. The great thing is that *anybody* can do it. All you need are a few basic skills and a tiny bit of effort. When you master it, the tables will turn: You'll learn to control your money instead of letting it control you.

WHY SHOULD YOU LEARN HOW TO BUDGET?

Let's explore a few reasons why budgeting is so important to your
financial success:

- A budget provides a clear, visual picture of where you
  stand financially each month.

- A budget helps you prioritize what really matters to you.

- A budget encourages you to be disciplined with your
  money and helps you save more of it.

- A budget presents a clearly organized plan that helps you
  remember which bills are due and when.

- A budget reflects the actual facts of your financial
  situation, rather than relying on assumptions about how
  well (or poorly) you're doing.

- A budget dictates how your money should work for you.

- A budget helps you "find" money you didn't know you had
  (or that you were spending unconsciously).

- A budget inspires you to live within your means.

- A budget presents actual, trackable, concrete results.

- Most importantly, a budget asserts *control over your
  money* and your life.

To zero down your debt, you must seize control over your money.
You need to have a plan. *You must tell your money what to do*. The
only way to do that is with a budget.

WHY BUDGETS FAIL

Many of us have attempted budgeting at some point in our lives. Unfortunately, most of us have also failed at it. There are a million reasons why budgets don't work out the way we would like. Here are a few of the most common reasons your past attempts may have been a flop:

You never really started, did you? The biggest reason budgets fail is that we never start budgeting in the first place. Maybe we're overwhelmed by what seems like a gigantic task. Maybe we're afraid to truly face the financial mess we are in. Maybe we worry it will require changes to our lives we don't want to make. So, we put it off and tell ourselves that we're going to start budgeting later... but we never do. *Start budgeting now.*

You never wrote anything down. Budgeting isn't something you can do in your head. It has to be written down. You need to be able to physically see the numbers and your progress. Budgeting in your head is a recipe for mistakes and disappearing paychecks. *Write your budget down.*

You mistake "budgeting" for something else. Sometimes, we think paying our bills and sticking to a budget are one and the same. Sorry, but that just isn't the case. Paying your bills on time is good financial practice, but it is not budgeting. It's just paying your bills. *Account for all your money each month, not just your bills.*

Your budget wasn't specific enough. Your budget won't work if you aren't being deliberate and specific with your money. Guessing can lead to overspending or deprivation, either of which can make you frustrated enough to give up. *Be as specific as you can.*

You didn't have an emergency fund. What happens when you don't have any savings and an unexpected expense pops up? You don't have the money to pay for it, and your budget is busted through no fault of your own. That leads to disappointment and giving up. *We'll teach you how to prevent this from happening by building an emergency fund.*

You never followed up. Once you've created your monthly budget, you still need to check in throughout the month. It takes less than five minutes a week. *Make sure your money is doing what you want it to by checking in regularly.*

You didn't commit. You can't tell us your budget didn't work if you didn't give it a chance. Until you decide that you really want to change, you haven't made the commitment to getting your money on track. *Make the decision to change your life.*

WHAT TOOLS DO YOU NEED?

The great thing about a budget is that it doesn't take a lot of equipment or expensive software to get started. All you need is a pen and paper.

Yep, that's it.

In fact, that's still what we use to this day.

Each month, we take about 15 minutes to create and review our budget. We bust out our spiral bound notebook, think about the month's expenses and income, and get to work jotting it down. It doesn't take long, but it's the most important money discussion we have each month. It's not fancy, but it works.

Notice that I said we do this *each month*. Why? ***Because it's that important***.

A budget is a living, breathing document. You have to create a new one every month. Each time the calendar flips, you'll have different expenses to account for. Sure, some of them are the same – like your mortgage or rent, internet bill, or car insurance – but many will change. You might attend a wedding in June, or maybe you're going on vacation in July. Your heating bill that was sky-high in March may be all but gone by April. Your budget needs to reflect these month-to-month changes, so it's *extremely* important that you update it every month.

So, grab that pen and paper and let's get down to business. It's time to zero down your debt by creating a Zero-Sum Budget!

HOW TO CREATE A BUDGET THAT ACTUALLY WORKS

Zero-Sum Budgeting: Zero Is the Goal

The budgeting strategy you're about to learn is called a **zero-sum budget**, sometimes referred to as zero-based budgeting. Once you learn our tips and tricks, you'll create a zero-based budget on a monthly basis.

To do this, you'll assign every single dollar you earn a *specific* purpose.

Remember Truth #5: When you tell your money what to do, it listens. It's almost like... magic!

The goal is to ensure that your income and expenses are *exactly balanced* – "zeroed out." This is so important, we're going to say this again:

Your income and your expenses should balance to the penny.

Here's the simple formula that makes it all work:

Income - Expenses - Savings = $0

BAM! Intention. Control. Success.

Easy-peasy, right?

OK, let's get started.

Step 1: Write it Down

As we mentioned earlier, a successful budget is one that is actually written down. This may not seem like a big deal, but it's the most crucial step in the budgeting process. So, let's repeat that one more time:

Your budget must be written down.

You might have a mind like a steel trap. We don't care. Keeping a budget in your head is a recipe for budgeting disaster. It's ripe for "abouts" and "close-tos" and other approximations. It's a prime strategy for forgetting about bills and underestimating their costs.

Your budget can't be a guess. Guessing leaves far too much room for error, which means money is going to disappear. You don't want that. You need to be exact.

With the exception of variable expenses (which we'll talk about shortly), you should pretty much know – to the penny – how much your bills cost each month. Unless you have a variable income (which we'll also discuss), you should know how much money you take home each month.

A written budget keeps track of all of that. By writing it down, you can positively see how much you have to spend and what you need to spend it on. Your budget must be written down, ***clearly***, so you can see it.

Write. It. Down.

Capiche?

Now, having a written budget can mean a lot of things. You can use a simple sheet of paper like we do. Of course, using a spreadsheet is fine, too. If you want to get super fancy, you can even use a budgeting app. It doesn't matter how you write it down. What matters is that it's somewhere you can physically see it... with your eyes! Visualizing doesn't count.

Step 2: Use Last Month's Income

If using a written budget is the most important step for success, this little trick is easily the second. It helps us know EXACTLY how much money is at our disposal. No guessing, remember?

OK, here it is:

Base your budget on last month's income.

TA-DA! There's a bit of magic to this simple piece of common sense.

If you've struggled to stay on budget in the past, using last month's income is going to be a game changer for you. It eliminates the guesswork!

If you're like most people, you don't pay your bills with any plan in mind. You spend according to your bank balance, not according to what you're earning. Without a plan, you THINK you still have money available for that month. You mistake "paying your bills" for "having a budget."

BUZZZZZZ! Wrong answer!

When you're guessing how much money you have, the entire foundation of your budget is built on assumptions. Estimates and approximations lead to spending money that isn't there. The next thing you know, you've rung up $700 in expenses that you can't cover. And when you can't cover your expenses with cash, you have to use debt to stay afloat.

Not with us. Not with a zero-sum budget.

We want you to be as exact as possible. So, instead of basing your budget on a guess, base it on your actual earnings.

> *"Don't budget according to what you think you have available. Base your budget on what you know you have. Base it on last month's take-home income instead!"*

Don't budget according to what you *think* you have available. Base your budget on what you *know* you have. Base it on last month's take-home income instead!

Now, the eventual goal with a zero-sum budget is to **keep one full month of expenses saved** so you can use that precise amount for the following month's budget. This is your "monthly expense cushion."

Look, we know this sounds like a dream. We realize you're probably thinking, "Yeah, right." Just trust us – we'll get there.

Saving up a month's worth of expenses may seem like an enormous hill to climb, but it isn't that difficult when you have the right tools. Once you start using a written zero-sum budget, saving that money becomes easy. It's just another part of your monthly plan. We'll explain how to do it in Step 4.

Let's start creating our "sample" written budget. At the top, **create a section for income**. Add up the total amount of income you took home over the last month, and jot down the number there.

Provided you haven't already spent it, this is the amount of money you have available. It should look something like this:

Income: $5,000

Draw a line underneath it, and move on to the next section.

Step 3: Determine Your Monthly Expenses

Back on your budget worksheet, create a new section for "**Monthly Expenses**." Stick it right under your monthly income from last month. Just plop it down on the page, and let's discuss.

Before we create separate categories for each expense, let's start by breaking them into two groups: *Fixed* and *Variable.*

Generally, fixed expenses cost you the same amount of money each month. You don't have a ton of control over how much they cost, but you do know how much you need to budget for them each month. Fixed expenses may include:

- Mortgage or rent
- Health, life, or car insurance premiums
- Cable
- Internet
- Phone
- Cell phone

- Student loan payments

- Car payments

- Understand that fixed expenses do not always mean *necessary* expenses. Some of them are optional. For example, you don't *have to* subscribe to cable TV. You're not required to pay premium prices for cell phone and data plans. You can cut these expenses out of your budget if necessary. *Fixed* simply means that the amount you owe doesn't change.

Add each fixed expense category to your Monthly Expenses section. Go over your most recent bills, and use them to determine how much money you should allocate this month toward each expense. Write it down.

Now, let's discuss variable expenses. These are expenses over which you have (almost) complete control. You can choose how much (or how little) to spend on each of these over the course of the month, and you can adjust those costs every month or as the need arises. Some types of variable expenses include:

- Utilities (such as gas or electricity)

- Groceries

- Entertainment

- Restaurant spending

- Credit cards

- Clothing

- Gas or other transportation

- Miscellaneous

Again, "variable" does not mean necessary. It simply means that the amount you owe can change from month to month. Don't confuse the two.

Budgeting for variable expenses can be a bit tricky, and it's one place people tend to get tripped up. Because these expenses are variable, we actually have to estimate their costs.

We want our estimate to be as close as possible to our actual cost. Last month's bills should give us a pretty good idea of how much to expect, so use that as a starting point. However, if we know our expenses might be higher this month, it's always best to estimate on the high side. That way, we don't have a shortfall in our budget. At worst, we can roll over the surplus into our savings and use it next month.

Let's repeat that one more time:

When estimating variable expenses, leave a buffer. Be sure your estimate is a little high.

It's always best to use a more conservative estimate. Instead of busting your budget with a shortfall, you'll have a surplus that can be used later.

Going back to your budget worksheet, add your variable expense categories to the Monthly Expenses section. Determine how much money you will allocate to each category. Your budget might now look something like this:

Income: $5,000

	Monthly Expenses
Mortgage:	$1,500
Utilities:	$150
Health insurance:	$500
Life insurance:	$25
Cable:	$102.80
Internet:	$45.73

Home Phone:	$34.13
Cell phone:	$93.38
Student loans:	$300
Car payments:	$425
Groceries:	$575
Entertainment:	$100
Restaurant spending:	$100
Credit card (minimums):	$100
Clothing:	$0
Miscellaneous:	$48.96
Total Expenses:	**$4,100**

Remember, you want to be specific and exact. You want to account for every single penny you earn and spend during the month!

> *"When you pay yourself first, you can't put it off."*

Step 4: Create a Plan for Savings and Debt Repayment

Here's where the fun really starts! This is where you're going to use to start zeroing down your debt and building your emergency fund (which will discuss in another chapter).

Later in the process, you'll create categories for savings vehicles like college savings plans, Individual Retirement Accounts (IRAs), and more. But, because we're, working to pay off debt, we need to prioritize that in our savings section for now. We're also guessing that you don't have an emergency fund to fall back on. So, you'll also use this category to stock your emergency fund until it's fully funded. (We'll discuss emergency funds in more detail in Chapter 6.)

Once you have your starter emergency fund in place and have paid off your debt, you can begin building your monthly expense buffer. You'll use the money you were putting toward your emergency fund and debt repayment to establish a buffer equivalent to one month's expenses. Then, you'll focus on fully funding your emergency fund and other long-term savings goals.

In order of importance, your savings goals should be:

- 1A) Beginner emergency fund (up to $1,000)

- 1B) Debt repayment (until paid off)

- 2) Monthly Expense Buffer (up to 1 month's expenses)

- 3) Fully-stocked emergency fund (three to six months of expenses)

- 4) Additional retirement, college savings, and other savings goals

Again, you're trying to unleash the power of your paycheck to achieve your biggest goals. Fund these goals *before* you spend on wants such as entertainment and new clothes. When you **pay yourself first**, you can't put it off. Money doesn't disappear into variable expenses like food or new Beyonce albums.

So, go ahead and add a savings section, then jot down each individual savings (or debt repayment) vehicle you're using. Decide how much money you want to save this month, and allocate it into your savings categories accordingly.

At this point, your entire zero-sum budget for the month should look something like this:

Income: $5,000

	Monthly Expenses
Mortgage:	$1,500
Utilities:	$150
Health insurance:	$500
Life insurance:	$25
Cable:	$102.80
Internet:	$45.73
Home Phone:	$34.13
Cell phone:	$93.38
Student loans:	$300
Car payments:	$425
Groceries:	$575
Entertainment:	$100
Restaurant spending:	$100
Credit card (minimums):	$100
Clothing:	$0
Miscellaneous:	$48.96
Total Expenses:	**$4,100**
Emergency fund:	$500

Debt repayment:	$400
Total Savings/Debt Repayment:	**$900**

Step 5: Review and Balance

Huzzah! The hard work is done. Now, we need to make sure that your budget zeros out. You remember our formula, right?

Income - Expenses - Savings = $0

Our example above balances perfectly:

$5,000 - $4,100 - $900 = $0

Everything you've put in your budget should balance out and equal zero. If it does, you're done! You've created a zero-sum budget.

If not, then...

What to Do if You Have a Negative Number: If you end up with a negative number, you have overspent. You'll need to make adjustments by cutting your expenses (preferable), cutting your savings (not preferable), or increasing your income. Once you've made the necessary adjustments, go back and run the equation again.

What to Do if You Have a Positive Number: If your equation balances to a positive number, congratulations! You have extra money in your budget!!! Quick, go stash that money into your savings or throw more of it at your debt before it disappears!

Step 6: Repeat Each Month

Yay! You've just completed your first monthly budget! Now that you've got the template down, use the same process to prepare your budget next month.

If your budget fell apart this month, don't worry. It may take a little bit of practice to get it right. We've all failed with our budget at one point or another, and we'll teach you how to handle disasters later in the book. The important thing is that you are now *on a budget*.

You are in control of the money you have. Keep at it, and you'll work out the kinks in no time.

HANDLING PAYMENTS UNTIL YOU HAVE AN EXPENSE CUSHION

As we've discussed, you eventually want to get to the point where you can budget an entire month of expenses and live off of your previous month's income. But, how the heck do you get to that point?

Here's the thing: You won't be able to start out basing your budget on last month's income. It's something you'll need to work up to. First, you need to work on building a beginner emergency fund and destroying your debt. Using the debt repayment techniques described later in the book, you'll destroy your debt at warp speed.

So, what do you do in the meantime?

Here's a little trick to help you out:

When you're creating your budget, you need to think in terms of the monthly picture. Regardless of whether you get paid once a month or receive multiple paychecks, you should know how much you take home on a monthly basis. Likewise, by using the zero-sum budgeting model above, you now know what your monthly expenses look like.

Until you can use last month's income to pay your expenses, you'll need to organize things a bit differently. In addition to creating a written zero-based budget like we described above, you'll want to assign each bill to a paycheck according to when they are due. Bills due at the beginning of the month should be come out of the first paycheck you earn each month. Bills due at the end of the month should be assigned to your mid-month paycheck. As your paychecks roll in each month, you'll want to pay bills and expenses according to your zero-sum budget plan.

The same is true about savings. If your budget says you should throw $250 toward savings each month, you should do exactly that – either in the beginning of the month or the end.

Wherever it makes sense and won't threaten overdrafting your account.

Over time, you'll build a stash big enough to use for an entire month's expenses. At that point, you'll just start sticking your paychecks in savings to use for the next month's budget. Once you have enough savings built up, you should be able to "pay yourself" exactly what you need to live on each month – using your last month's income for the current month's expenses.

Remember, living off last month's income takes the guesswork out of the equation. You don't have to estimate how much you'll earn or spend; you already know.

HOW TO BUDGET FOR A VARIABLE INCOME

The process outlined above works great, especially if you have a relatively steady income. But, not everybody earns their paycheck in a straight line.

Salespeople who work on commissions, self-employed business owners, freelancers, seasonal workers... if you work in one of these jobs, you know how tough it can be to plan for the monthly income swings. One month, you're swimming in cash while the next you're broke as a joke.

So, what can you do? Just throw in the towel, swear off budgeting all together, and call it quits?

You know the answer to that.

While it's true that budgeting for a variable income is a bit trickier, it's not impossible. Not even close. When your income goes through wild swings, it's more important than ever to have a budget that works. Here's how to do it.

First, you need to understand what your most important monthly expenses are. Just so you don't have to guess, we'll lay them out for you:

- Food

- Shelter

- Utilities

- Transportation

Why are these the most important? You need food to live. You need a home to live in, with heat, water, and electricity. Finally, you need a way to get to work so that you can make money.

Make sense? Let's do this.

Take out a sheet of paper and list your expense categories from most to least important. Start with the top four, and work your way down. Each month you get paid, "spend" the money from your paycheck to cover each category, just like you would with the zero-sum budget we explained earlier.

Your ultimate goal is to get on the zero-sum budget described earlier. The hard part is finding a way to even out your income so it stays relatively stable each month. If you have the money, an easy way to do that is to implement what we call a **"Boom and Bust Account."**

The idea behind the Boom and Bust Account is to stash extra money away during the "boom" times, and draw money from the account in the "bust" times. This account calms those wild swings in "available income" each month. Here's how it works.

Let's say you make about $18,000 in take-home commission pay every three months, which averages $6,000 a month in income. Let's also assume that you owe $4,000 in expenses each month, which leaves you with an average of $2,000 to squirrel away each month for additional retirement and savings.

Although you make an average of $6,000 a month, the cash flow is rarely distributed evenly. In January, you might take home $18,000, while in February and March you might earn zilch.

So, in January, keep $6,000 of your $18,000 paycheck to pay yourself and your bills for that month. Then, assume you won't be paid again for another three months. Take the additional $12,000 and put it in your Boom and Bust Account. If you only make $1,000 in February, withdraw $5,000 from the account to pay your bills and your savings. Do the same for March, if needed. When you get another big check in April, save $6,000 for your monthly bills and replenish the Boom and Bust Account with the rest.

Any time you get the chance, fill your account back up to the proper level. A good rule of thumb is to know how often, on average, you get paid. If you know you usually get paid every three months, you should have three months' worth of budget money stashed in your Boom & Bust Account. If you work a seasonal job, you need enough to cover the seasons when you aren't working.

You know better than anybody the variations in your pay schedule, so you need to decide how much should stay in the account.

Here's another example:

You know that you may make about $60,000 from March to November and only $10,000 from December to March. That's an average of $5,833 per month, which is great! But, here's the problem. You only average $2,500 a month for four months of the year. Thus, you have a monthly shortfall of $3,333 over a four-month period.

So what do you do?

You need enough in your Boom and Bust Account to make up the difference. In this case, a fully funded Boom and Bust Account would have $13,332 in it: $3,333 shortfall x 4 months = $13,332 needed in B&B Account.

That means from March through November, you need to add extra money to your Boom and Bust Account to fill the gap. If that money comes in evenly, you should add $1,666.50 each month ($13,332/8 months).

If the money you make comes in sporadically from the spring through the fall, simply assume your average monthly income is $5,833 per month. Anything you make above that needs to go into the Boom and Bust Account until you reach the full $13,332. So, if you make $10,000 in June, you should put $4,167 of it into the Boom and Bust Account. *Capiche?*

Keep in mind that this account needs to stay separated from your other savings accounts. It's not meant for savings, and it is not your emergency fund. This is a separate account that you're using *only* to balance the swings in your income. It is not for *anything* else.

Budgeting this way takes a little bit of extra work. But, once you master this skill and use your Boom & Bust Account accordingly, you'll find yourself spending more deliberately and saving more money.

ACTION ITEMS

Here's what you should be doing now:

At the beginning of next month (or toward the very end of this month), create your own zero-sum budget.

Make sure you write it down so that you can see it.

Check in with your budget a few times a week to make sure that you're staying on track. Adjust your budget as needed.

At the end of the month, look for any improvements or tweaks you can make. Rinse and repeat!

NOTES

_____

_____

_____

_____

_____

_____

_____

_____

_____

_____

_____

_____

NOTES

NOTES

_____

_____

_____

_____

_____

_____

_____

_____

_____

_____

_____

NOTES

NOTES

_____

_____

_____

_____

_____

_____

_____

_____

_____

_____

_____

_____

CHAPTER 4

Executing Your Budget and Tracking the Results

In this chapter you'll learn:

- Why debt doesn't discriminate by income

- The root cause of debt

- How to track your spending

- Why tracking your spending is crucial if you hope to remain debt-free

- How to compare your actual spending with the numbers on your written budget

- Tips and tricks that can help you track and reduce your spending each month

Congratulations! You've completed your first monthly budget. High fives all around!

As you know, a budget is a monthly plan for your money. It lays the groundwork, telling your dollars where to go and what to do. It's the foundation of good money management and the key to harnessing the power of your paycheck so you can get out of debt.

But, without action, a plan is just a plan. And plans can change... and sometimes we forget our plans... and sometimes we ignore them altogether.

So, how do we handle that? How do we make sure our plan is working?

We need a reliable way to stay on track, to ensure our careful planning is bearing the fruit we intended. We need a results-oriented system that presents a clear picture of our *actual* spending behaviors versus what we intend to spend. We need to track our spending.

WHAT IS TRACKING YOUR SPENDING?

Tracking your spending is the sidekick to your monthly budget. It's the Robin to your budget's Batman. The Laurel to your budget's Hardy. The JLo to your... well, you get the picture. It goes hand-in hand with your budget, delivering the data you need to whip your money into shape.

To track our spending, we'll use a simple system that records what we spend every month. We'll group each expense, both individually and by category, so we know *exactly* how much money we're spending... and on what. Then, we'll compare it to our budget to confirm we're spending according to our plan.

THE IMPORTANCE OF TRACKING YOUR SPENDING

Let's start off with a question: Who's better off in the long run, a doctor making $200,000 a year who spends all of it, or a plumber who makes $60,000 a year and saves 25% of his income?

The answer should be easy. If you spend every penny you make, you're just as broke as if you made nothing at all. You might accumulate a lot of junk, but you're not building wealth. You're just spinning your wheels.

> *"You can't zero down your debt with more money alone, you have to fix the root cause. You must control your spending. Remember, you probably have all that you need already. You just need to manage it properly."*

Debt isn't just for people with low or average incomes. High earners can find themselves broke and deep in debt too. Maybe you're a high earner and find yourself reading this book. If you are, there's no shame in that. Let's figure out how to unleash the power of your paycheck and get you back on the right foot. Luckily for you, there's plenty of power hidden in that income.

We've all heard about professional athletes who went bankrupt or millionaires who mismanaged their money and ended up broke, right? It happens all the time. And it has nothing to do with the *amount* of money they make – it has everything to do with *how they spend it.*

It's easy to confuse income with wealth. It's even easier to confuse high-dollar spending with wealth. Neither is true.

Yes, bigger paychecks are great, but they don't cure the root cause of debt. Whether you're a business mogul or a laborer, earning more money only does one thing: It gives you the *opportunity* to get ahead. In the end, it's what you do with that opportunity that counts.

You can't zero down your debt with more money alone, you have to fix the root cause. You must control your spending. Remember, you probably have all that you need already. You just need to manage it properly.

That brings us to this truth:

TRUTH #7:

Debt neither discriminates nor is cured by income. Rather, it is caused and controlled by spending.

When you control your spending, it doesn't really matter how much money you make. There are exceptions, of course, but this is true for the vast majority of people. Learning to live on a budget means you always have more money coming in than going out. We call this "living within your means," and it's a simple but seriously effective tool for creating disposable income – income we're going to use to pay off debt.

But where do you start? To control your spending, you need to know what you're spending money on, and how much. That's where tracking your expenses comes in. So, let's look at what this technique can do for you.

5 WAYS TRACKING YOUR SPENDING HELPS YOU GET OUT OF DEBT

Tracking your expenses helps you:

- Know exactly how much you're spending – and on what
- Find "spending leaks" in your budget
- Stick to your budget
- Live within your means
- Understand the consequences of your spending behaviors

Knowing Your Expenses: Destroying your debt requires brutal honesty about your spending habits. You can't get ahead financially if you're spending more money than you make each month. Like with budgeting, the devil is often in the details. By tracking your spending, you'll know exactly where all of your money is going –

every last penny. And, once you know *how* you're spending, it's far easier to make the adjustments needed to get out of debt.

Finding "Spending Leaks" in Your Budget: Once you know where your money is going, you can easily find any gaps in your budget that need to be plugged. Maybe you're forgetting to budget for your cell phone bill, or maybe you aren't factoring in enough for groceries. Maybe you set aside $20 a month for coffee and snacks, but on closer inspection, those trips to the coffee shop or convenience store take a bigger bite out of your budget than you realized. By consistently tracking your spending, you'll know how to tweak your budget so it actually works.

Staying on Budget: Tracking your spending also helps you stick to your budget throughout the month. By keeping a current tally of expenditures, you'll know exactly where you stand at any moment. Simply compare your expense tracker with your budget every week to make sure you're on track. If you've overspent in one category, cut back in another so it balances out. This only takes a few minutes each week, but it can make all the difference.

Living Within Your Means: By tracking your expenses, you don't have to make guesses or assumptions about where you might be overspending. The numbers are right there on the page. Tracking your spending also provides a great starting point for determining which expenses are necessary and which aren't. To get out of debt fast, you'll need to identify and cut some of those more frivolous expenses. Once you do, you won't just be living *within* your means, you'll be living *below* them. (We'll teach you how in the next chapter!)

Understanding the Consequences of Spending: When you track your spending, you have a clear, specific, honest picture about how you are *actually* handling your money. There is nowhere to run, nowhere to hide. There are no excuses or estimates or *woulda-coulda-shouldas*. The cold hard numbers are there on the page, staring you blankly in the face. This is your behavior, like it or not. It's a true record of what you spent, and it helps you confront that reality. Once you understand the truth, you have a choice: Continue your reckless spending, or implement the changes necessary to get out of debt.

OUR AH-HA MOMENT

One of the most important moments in our personal journey out of debt came when we started tracking our expenses. We sat down and took an objective look at how we'd been handling our money. What we found shook us to the core.

We were making plenty of money, and we really *thought* we were living a frugal lifestyle. We didn't buy new clothes, we only bought things on sale, and we used a coupon whenever we could. We weren't struggling, but we weren't saving either – blowing through our paychecks without ever really knowing why or how.

But, sometimes the things we *think* to be true are proven wrong by the facts. Even though we *thought* we were frugal, tracking our expenses helped us understand and identify the *fact* that we weren't. We were overspending, even if we didn't want to believe it.

Before we started, we expected to find certain overindulgences. We knew we were spending too much on junk like cable TV and car payments. But, we actually found other expenses we didn't realize were affecting our bottom line. One of the biggest was food costs. We were eating away our savings and didn't even know it!

Seriously, we were shocked. How could we be spending over $1,000 a month on food for two adults? $1,000 a month?!? That couldn't be.

But, it was. And it was right there on paper for both of us to see.

It was a moment that changed our lives. We had to make a choice: We could continue risking our financial future by ignoring our out-of-control spending habits, or we could change our ways.

You know what our decision was. How will you choose?

HOW TO TRACK YOUR SPENDING

As with budgeting, tracking your expenses doesn't require fancy spreadsheets or high-tech software. All you really need to get started is a pen and a couple of sheets of paper... so go and grab them!

Now that you're ready, create a simple table on each sheet. One table will be your "Expense Register," and the other you'll use to categorize each expense.

Let's start with the Expense Register. Create two columns and draw a line down the middle. Label the column on the left as "Expenses" and the one on the right as "Amount." When you're done, your chart should look something like this:

MONTHLY EXPENSE REGISTER*

EXPENSES	AMOUNT

* Protracted charts can be found at the end of the book.

Boom. Easy right?

Over the next 30 days, every time you make a purchase, record what you bought and how much it cost. To ensure accuracy, do this on daily basis. Write it **all** down, even that $1.25 you spent on gas station mints. No cheating!

Remember, your paycheck is the most powerful wealth building tool at your disposal. Every penny you spend matters because each purchase decreases its power. Therefore, you want to be as accurate as you possibly can. You must account for every expenditure, especially at first when you're struggling to get on track. If you aren't accurate or honest with yourself, you can't find the problems.

Now, let's design your other table. Label it "Monthly Spending by Category." Again, create two columns with a line down the middle. Label the left side as "Expense Categories" and the right side as "Total Spent." It should look like this:

MONTHLY SPENDING BY CATEGORY*

EXPENSES	AMOUNT

Next, create categories for each expense you typically incur during the month. These categories should be the same categories you listed on your monthly budget. Some examples may include mortgage or rent, utilities, groceries, cable TV, internet, cell phone service, telephone service, entertainment, health insurance, life insurance, savings, retirement savings, car payment, car insurance, gas, miscellaneous, etc.

Once you've done that, add them to your table under Expense Categories.

MONTHLY SPENDING BY CATEGORY

EXPENSE CATEGORIES	TOTAL SPENT
Mortgage/Rent	
Utilities	
Groceries	
Gas	
Restaurants	
Savings	
Retirement	
Cable TV	
Cell Phone	
Internet	
Telephone	
Health Insurance	
Life Insurance	
Car Payment	
Car Insurance	
Entertainment	
Miscellaneous	

At the end of the month, go through your Expense Register and add up everything you spent. The amount is your "Total Spending."

Now, move back to your "Monthly Spending by Category" table. Starting with the first category, compare it to your Expense Register. Add up all the expenses that fall into each category. Once you've counted an expense on your register, place a checkmark next to it so you don't include it twice. When you have a total for that category, write it down in the "Total Spent" column of your Monthly Spending by Category table. Repeat this for each category.

Some categories will only have one or two entries, while others may have several. Chances are you only make one mortgage payment a month, but you might go to the grocery store four or five times. Just add them all up, and check off each item once you've accounted for it.

When you're done, all of the expenses on your Expense Register should have a checkmark next to them. As you come across random purchases, put them in "Miscellaneous" or add more categories to your table as needed. Your chart should now look something like this:

Expense Categories	Total Spent
Mortgage/Rent	$1,200.00
Utilities	300.51
Groceries	751.65
Gas	103.11
Restaurants	250.23
Savings	100.00
Retirement	400.00
Cable TV	167.50
Cell Phones	125.00
Internet	35.79

Telephone	25.21
Health Insurance	745.00
Life Insurance	50.00
Car Payment	505.16
Car Insurance	104.23
Entertainment	300.00
Miscellaneous	297.05

Now, add each entry in the "Total Spent" column to get a grand total. It should match the grand total from your expense register. Once you've done that, write it down and you're done! You've just tracked your expenses.

COMPARING YOUR RESULTS

Now that you've tracked your spending for an entire month, you've got the raw data needed to tighten up your budget. It's time to compare your monthly budget – what you *want* to be spending – to what you *actually* spent. Ideally, the amount you spent on each category should mirror the amount you allotted in your budget.

If the numbers match, you nailed it. You're on budget! If your expenses are less than what you budgeted, you still win. You're under budget! Quick, go chuck that money at your debt and do a victory dance.

However, if your expense totals are higher than what you budgeted for, you went over. It's OK. Don't beat yourself up over it. Few of us get things right on the first try.

Remember, one of the main reasons we track our spending is to find holes in our budget. We can't repair them if we don't know where they are. So, in that way, it's still a success! Figure out where you went over and why. Then, make adjustments so you can do better next month.

Tips & Tricks for Tracking Your Spending

Be Accurate: Strive to be as accurate as possible. You want to know exactly where your money is actually going. The first few times you track your spending, you may find that you don't know where some of it went. That's OK. Simply categorize it as "I Don't Know" and aim to get that number down to zero.

Do a Weekly Check-In: Don't just compare your budget and expense tracking at the end of the month. Compare your results at least once per week. This simple exercise will help you identify issues and make adjustments on the fly, giving you a better shot at staying on budget throughout the month.

Record Expenses Daily: When you're first starting out, it's a great idea to record your expenses on a daily basis. Just take three or four minutes to jot down what you spent that day. It will improve your accuracy, making it easier to find spending problems.

Use the Same Categories: When creating your expense categories, use the same categories you've already used on your monthly budget. This makes it easier to compare your planned spending with your real-world results.

Include Debt Repayment: Be sure to leave a spot for your debt repayment. This won't show up the first time you track your expenses, but leave room for it after you start budgeting. Remember, you want to use any extra or "found" money to zero down your debts each month! Account for your baseline repayment on your budget and when tracking your expenses.

Be Kind to Yourself: Like with budgeting, be kind to yourself. When you're tracking your spending, you're simply gathering the raw data so you can see where you stand. It's OK that you've made bad spending decisions in the past. The important thing is to discover and change those behaviors.

ACTION ITEMS

Let's recap what you should do now:

Start tracking your expenses today. Then, start clean on the first day of the month by writing down each purchase and expense.

If you have a record of last month's expenses (bank statements, receipts, and credit card bills), you can use those documents to analyze your spending from last month instead. Bust out a piece of paper and your bank statement. Now, go through all of your expenses from last month and write them down. If you don't know where some of the money went, that's OK. Categorize it as "I Don't Know" and try to zero that down next month. Repeat each month.

NOTES

_____

_____

_____

_____

_____

_____

_____

_____

_____

_____

_____

_____

NOTES

_____

_____

_____

_____

_____

_____

_____

_____

_____

_____

_____

NOTES

_____

_____

_____

_____

_____

_____

_____

_____

_____

_____

_____

NOTES

_____

_____

_____

_____

_____

_____

_____

_____

_____

_____

_____

_____

CHAPTER 5

Analyzing Your Spending, Eliminating Waste, and Avoiding Budget Vampires

In this chapter you'll learn:

- How to analyze your spending and eliminate waste

- Why "live below your means" is the best advice of all

- How to define your wants and needs

- How to say "no" so that you can say "yes"

- Common budget vampires and how to avoid them

Tracking your spending isn't only about the numbers. It's about gathering information and making changes if needed. We've talked about how small changes can lead to big results. When it comes to destroying your debt, the biggest change you can make is through drastically cutting your expenses.

> *"Most of us have more than enough money to purchase the things and experiences that are important to us. So why does money feel so tight? It's because we waste the money we already have on things that don't matter. We use our paychecks inefficiently".*

We know, we know. Nobody wants to hear that they're living beyond their means. We all want *what* we want, *when* we want it. Anything else feels like a sacrifice, which is generally something we're not willing to make.

But it's not a sacrifice. Not really, anyway. Stick with us here.

Most of us have more than enough money to purchase the things and experiences that are important to us. So why does money feel so tight? It's because we waste the money we already have on things that don't matter. We use our paychecks inefficiently.

Although we don't think twice about it, grabbing a mocha latte, hitting a restaurant for lunch, and paying for gadgets we don't need impacts more than just our bottom line. It affects the way we're able to live our lives. We spend without thinking, and it crushes our ability to save. But, instead of cutting back on impulse buys, we surrender to the urges of instant gratification. Instead of saving for what we really want, we mindlessly spend on whatever tickles our fancy at that exact moment. We choose the quickly fleeting pleasure of now above the long-term satisfaction and *real* happiness that saving for our goals can deliver.

Winning the game of money is about making choices. And whether or not you're conscious of your spending choices, you're still choosing. Being deliberate with your money and making conscious spending decisions means *you* are in control. Spending without purpose means you're not.

Don't confuse making choices with sacrifice. Choosing to reduce your spending is not the same thing as deprivation. In fact, it can provide a tremendous boost to your long-term financial goals. Just cut the waste and reap the rewards.

For example, let's suppose you spend an average of $15 eating lunch with your coworkers each day. That's pretty easy to do – it's just lunch, right?

Well, $15 per weekday totals about $75 per week, or around $300 a month. By cutting back just a little – say, just getting two light lunches or one dinner out each week – you'll only spend an average of $25 a week. That means you'll save $200 a month. Do that for five months, and you've "found" an extra thousand bucks laying around! Live that way for a year, and you've effectively given yourself a $2,600 raise!

What could you do with that money? How could an extra $2,600 help destroy your debt and change your life? Remember, this is *your* money. It's money you already have at your disposal, and you can save it all by making one simple change. Heck, you don't even have to cut it all out! Just eat out less and you've unleashed $2,600 worth of power in your own paycheck!

This is just *one* spending choice. Think about what could happen if you made small cuts like this in two or three places. You'd have thousands of dollars at your disposal – money you can use to pay off debt, meet your savings goals, and get what you really want!

That brings us to our next fundamental truth:

TRUTH #8:

Living below your means is the most efficient way to unleash your paycheck's powerful potential.

So far, we've talked about getting on a budget and living within our means. But if we really want to make a change – if we *really* want to destroy our debt and seize control of our life – we need to do more than just live *within* our means. We need to live **below** our means.

See how that works?

Remember, we can make enormous changes with small steps. By cutting unnecessary expenses and living below our means, we unlock the potential of our paycheck to save, destroy debt, and live life on our own terms. Then, we harness that potential by using a budget, putting money toward our priorities, and paying off our debt at warp speed. It's all coming together nicely, right?

WHAT IT MEANS TO "LIVE BELOW YOUR MEANS"

Living below your means doesn't mean you have to go without. It doesn't mean you have to live like a pauper. It just means you save more than you spend – that you have more money coming in than going out. What a novel concept, right?

Most of us live life upside down. We live beyond our means, caving to our every desire, spending more than we make. Of course, that's how we get ourselves into debt. *When we spend more than we make, we have to use money we don't have to buy things we can't afford.* That's no way to live, and our behavior always catches up with us... eventually.

Living below your means takes a different mindset, but it only requires a small adjustment. To get there, we must find ways to control and cut our spending. Luckily for us, the hard work is already done. Everything we need to know is right there in our expense tracking worksheets. So, let's take a look at how to analyze the data we've been collecting.

ANALYZING YOUR SPENDING

Remember Truth #7? It says, "Debt neither discriminates nor is cured by income. Rather, it is caused and controlled by spending."

So, let's learn how to control it.

To make the biggest and quickest impact on our finances, it's best to start with the low-hanging fruit. In this case, it's overspending.

How do we know if we're overspending? Here are three basic ways we overspend in our daily lives:

- Overspending on our budget
- Borrowing money
- Overcommitting our paycheck

Let's discuss each in a bit more detail.

OVERSPENDING ON YOUR BUDGET

Spending more than you planned on a certain budget category is fairly common – especially at first. To determine if this is a problem in your life, compare your expense tracking sheet to your budget. If you've spent more money than you allocated in the budget, you've overspent.

If it's a simple mistake of not budgeting enough for that expense, try to be more accurate. Better yet, overestimate next month. On the other hand, if you feel like you spent more than you'd want to, keep a closer eye on your expenses throughout the following month. A weekly check-in with your budget should help do the trick.

OVERSPENDING BY BORROWING

Overspending by borrowing is also pretty straightforward. When you're trying to cut wasteful spending from your life, look at all the ways you're living beyond your means. The next time you're ready to buy something, here are two simple questions that can help:

- *Can I pay cash for this?*
- *Have I planned for this expense in my monthly budget?*
- If the answer to both is "yes," you can afford it. If you've answered "no" to either, you can't; and, if you decide to charge the item using

credit anyway, *you're using money you don't have to buy something you can't afford.* By definition, you are living beyond your means. Stop. Just stop.

To be clear, let's use Truth #9 to phrase it a different way:

Truth #9:

If you can't pay cash, you can't afford it.

We know that sounds harsh. Lots of others will tell you otherwise. You'll find a million excuses and rationalizations to get around this... but it's true. If you don't have the cash for something, you cannot afford it. Not using cash is how you ran up debt in the first place.

Look, using cash can be difficult. Paying for items in full can be painful. As human beings, we naturally try to avoid pain. It hurts, we don't like it, and we go out of our way to dodge it.

But pain can actually be a good thing. Pain is a warning sign. It's meant to protect us from harming ourselves. It tells us, "STOP DOING THAT!" and – most of the time – we should listen.

Making purchases with cash hurts... and, it should. That pain helps us decide whether we *really* want what we are buying. It protects us from overspending, debt, and financial disaster.

Using debt dulls the sensation. It hides or delays the pain. It's like taking heavy painkillers to mask an injury before playing in the big game. You may get what you want now, but you can do serious damage that has long-term consequences... all because you don't realize that you're injuring yourself further.

Don't mask your money problems with debt. *Pay in cash, or use your debit card as a way to pay with cash from your bank account.* Use pain as a guide to help you avoid overspending. That goes for everything you buy – cars, furniture, cable TV. If you're borrowing money for anything above and beyond buying a house, you can't afford it. You are overspending. Period.

OVERCOMMITTING YOUR PAYCHECK

Of course, having the money to buy something doesn't mean you should. If you bought everything you could afford, you'd soon find that you can no longer afford much. You may be living at or within your means, but there's only so much money in the pot. When you spend every penny you make, you certainly aren't able to save or dig your way out of debt.

In today's world, there are so many ways to spend your money. We have gadgets and gizmos galore. There are cable TV packages with enticing add-ons and ever-smarter phones with data plans. We commit our paychecks to monthly subscriptions, gym memberships, and online purchasing clubs. But when your money is already spoken for, you don't have anything left to save or spend.

Here's the thing: Every spending decision you make has
- consequences. **When you use your money to purchase one item, it means you can't use it to buy something else.** You're making a
- choice, a choice stating that item A is more important than item B. And when you continually choose to fund A, B, and C, you have no money left for D.

Unfortunately, too many of us fail to recognize the consequences of these choices. Instead, we commit a large portion of our monthly paychecks to avoidable expenses.

As you'll recall, Truth #2 states: "Your paycheck is your most powerful wealth building tool." But each spending choice you make – particularly toward ongoing monthly subscriptions and bills – commits part of your earnings. Every expense reduces the power of your paycheck to buy the things you really want. You may be overcommitted and not even know it.

WANTS VS. NEEDS

When looking for places to cut spending, it helps to differentiate between our wants and needs. This should be pretty simple, right? Our "needs" constitute the things we need to live – food, shelter, basic clothing, water, utilities. Everything else is a want. Easy peasy.

Not so fast. Many believe some of our wants are actually needs. We convince ourselves that we'd never get by without them. This type of thinking is dangerous, and it can negatively impact the power of our paycheck.

Having a cell phone is a major convenience, but do you really *need* it? Cable TV is fun, but you don't need it to get by. The expensive preschool, the new car, the club sports – no matter what you're telling yourself – these are all wants. You *choose* to spend your money on these items, and that's OK. It also means you can make the choice to eliminate these costs.

Don't fool yourself into thinking your wants are needs. They aren't. And when you're scrambling to get out of debt, every expense you don't absolutely need is something to consider cutting. Capiche?

SAYING "NO" SO YOU CAN SAY "YES"

> *"We ought to spend money on the things we value. We trade our time – our lives – to earn money. So, when we trade our money to make a purchase, we're effectively trading part of our life to get it"*

That brings us to our next fundamental truth:

Truth #10:

Your spending decisions have consequences and are a reflection of your values.

We ought to spend money on the things we value. We trade our time – our lives – to earn money. So, when we trade our money to make a purchase, we're effectively trading part of our life to get it. What's more valuable than that?

If your spending doesn't reflect what you value, you need to make a change. You need to cut your wasteful spending. Start saying "no" to things that don't matter, so you can say "yes" to things that do. Stop spending and start living.

Comb through your budget and expense tracking worksheets. Take a look at the choices you're making. Are they solid, money-saving choices, or are they robbing resources that could be spent on what you truly want? How many of the expenses you consider "needs" are actually "wants"? What do your spending choices say about your values?

Let's look at an example: Many of us choose to spend $150 to $200 a month on cable television. That means we're paying around $2,000 a year JUST for TV. On the other hand, you may think you don't have the money to take a vacation this year. While you might give lip service to a desire for travel, your spending says otherwise. By choosing to spend money on your pricey TV package, you're effectively saying that you value TV more than a vacation.

Here's an even more extreme example: Perhaps you're struggling to put food on the table. You're also spending $200 a month on cell phone plans for the family. By choosing to keep your cell phone plans or refusing to scale them back, you're saying that cell service is more important than food. That is your spending decision. Those are your values.

Little expenses add up, too. Maybe you're spending $7 a day on coffee and a bagel each morning. That's about $2,500 a year spent on this one habit alone. That's real money, right down the drain. What dream is this habit costing you? Imagine what you could do if you stopped spending on things that didn't matter and started using that money on things you *really* want.

Cutting down on wants isn't the only way to fix your spending problem. Look for ways to spend less on legitimate needs as well. Negotiate your electric bill, turn the heat down, use less water. It all adds up. It all matters.

Realize that this doesn't have to be all or nothing. You don't need 250 cable TV channels, but you don't have to live without television either. In fact, you could cut the cord to cable, buy a Roku box, and get all the TV you want from Netflix and Hulu Plus for about $20 a month. (If you're paying $150 a month, that's a savings of over $1,500 a year!) You don't have to toss your cell phone, either. Pare down your data allowance or sign up for a discount cell phone plan and save thousands of dollars a year.

You don't have to go cold turkey. Just use your money more efficiently.

Also, keep in mind that it doesn't have to stay this way for forever. Once you've scraped your way out of debt, you might add a few of these optional expenditures back into your budget.

Remember Truth #8: "Living below your means is the most efficient way to unleash your paycheck's powerful potential." By making conscious choices about your spending, you have the power to change your financial life forever. Think about each purchase before you make it, and only buy things you can pay for with cash on hand. Saying "no" so you can say "yes" unleashes the power of your paycheck to destroy debt, build real wealth, and get the things you really want.

BEWARE OF BUDGET VAMPIRES

Everybody's journey to debt freedom is different, but – in many ways – it's the same. We all experience some common pitfalls and problems, and one of them is giving in to **Budget Vampires**.

Seriously, these monsters are as creepy as they sound. If you've got goose bumps... good! You need to avoid these bad boys.

So, what are they? Budget Vampires are expenses that suck the life from your budget, draining your accounts one dollar at a time. Some are obvious, some are not. Some we've touched on already, others not so much. Beware! These monsters can wreak havoc on your monthly saving and debt repayment plans.

Some common budget vampires include:

Car Payments: Nothing destroys your paycheck like a hefty car payment. You're in double trouble – overcommitting your paycheck AND overspending through borrowing. Want to buy a car? Pay cash for it, plain and simple.

If you already have a car payment, get out of it ASAP. If you can't pay it off within a few months, reassess your car situation and buy a cheaper car... with cash.

High-Interest Credit Card Debt: Ugh. High-interest credit card debt can drain your paycheck and destroy your financial plan. We'll talk about ways to eliminate this at warp speed in Chapter 7.

High-Interest Mortgage Rates: Mortgage rates are still super low. If your rate is over 4%, you could be losing serious money every month. Look into refinancing right away.

High-Interest Student Loans: Student loan payments can be brutal. Consider shopping around to refinance your private loans, but be careful. By privately refinancing a federal loan, you can lose some important government benefits.

Furniture and Appliances: Ah, financing. You gotta love the whole "12 months, same as cash" game... especially if you're a bank. Financing your furniture is just like financing a car.
You may not pay interest for a year, but you're still overcommitting your paycheck AND overspending through borrowing. Don't fall for this game. Pay cash.

Cable TV: The cost of cable TV has gotten outrageous. Why pay $150 a month when you only watch a handful of channels? Consider cutting the cord and using that savings to pay off your debt!

Cell Phone Service: This budget vampire is one of the new money suckers on the block. Paying ridiculous amounts for cell service and data plans isn't necessary, especially if you're struggling with debt. Consider a low-cost cell provider instead. In many cases, you can get the same services for half the price.

Expensive Hobbies: Everybody needs to relax, but have you consider what your favorite hobbies are costing you? Golf, sporting events, even scrapbooking – these things cost a lot of money. Check your expense tracking sheets, and look for expensive hobbies that could be eating up your disposable income.

Overpriced Daycares and Preschools: We all want the best for our kids, but is that expensive daycare or preschool really worth it? The mortgage payment you send to your kid's preschool each month isn't getting them into Harvard. And, if you keep spending money like this, you won't be able to afford it anyway. Look for a cheaper alternative where the kids are still safe and able to have fun, even if the toys aren't as high-tech. Save that money in a college fund instead. Your child will be far better off.

Kids' Activities: Here's another biggie. Youth sports and activities are no longer all about fun and teamwork. They are big business. From year-round soccer teams to traveling baseball leagues, these activities don't just cost you big bucks to enroll. There's also travel expenses plus the cost of your time to consider. And for what? The money you're spending chasing a rare full-ride scholarship could be saved in a college fund and used to pay for college on your own. Just remember, to pay for salaries and facilities, a LOT of kids need to be funneled through the program. Your kid doesn't have to be one of them.

Clothing: Yes, clothes are a need. But oh, fashion. So contrived, yet so important to far too many people. Fashion is one of the most ridiculous and expensive budget vampires around. Every season, there's a new look... and a new way to drain your budget dry. The only way to win is to not play.

Eating Out: This is an easy trap to fall into. We used to spend hundreds of dollars every month eating out, and it was killing our savings rate. By saving the money you spend at restaurants – even cheap fast-food joints – you could probably save hundreds of dollars a month. What could you do with that money? (Hint: Pay off your debt first!)

Banking Fees: Have you looked through your bank statement lately? You should. Be sure that your bank account isn't being sucked dry by fees. Minimum balance fees, account maintenance fees, and overdraft fees are just a few to look for. You're already behind, so why pay more than you should?

Retirement Account Fees: Although saving for retirement is beyond the scope of this book, we want you to be aware of the fees you might be incurring through your retirement program. Make sure you know how much you're paying for the opportunity to invest.

Overpriced Insurance Premiums: Check your bills to make sure you're getting the best insurance rates available. At least once a year, do a little price shopping to see if you can get a better deal.

That's a pretty scary list, right?

Luckily, you've got the tools to defeat these budget vampires. By using your budget and expense tracker, you can easily find leaks in your financial plan. Bust out your garlic and wooden stakes, and hunt down these budget vampires immediately!

ACTION ITEMS

Here's what you should do now:

Commit yourself to living below your means. Look for ways to say "no" to what you don't *really* want so you can say "yes" to the things you do. Stop spending. Start living.

Compare your budget and expense tracking worksheets. Are there areas where you're overspending? Make adjustments as needed.

Comb through your list of expenses and define your wants and needs. Which items do you really need? Which can you do without? Which wants are you convincing yourself you need? Look for ways to reduce your spending, hunt down your budget vampires, and cut them out.

Are you still buying things on credit? Stop. Each time you make a purchase, ask yourself if you have the cash to pay for it. Remember, if you can't pay cash, just say no. You can't afford it.

Use the money you're saving on unnecessary expenses and apply it to your debt. Pay it off as quickly as possible.

NOTES

NOTES

_____

_____

_____

_____

_____

_____

_____

_____

_____

_____

_____

_____

NOTES

_____

_____

_____

_____

_____

_____

_____

_____

_____

_____

_____

NOTES

_____

_____

_____

_____

_____

_____

_____

_____

_____

_____

_____

_____

CHAPTER 6

When Things Go Wrong:
How to Survive the Unexpected

In this chapter you'll learn:

- How to survive a budget meltdown

- The importance of an emergency fund

- How to start and grow your own emergency fund

- Other common budgeting mistakes and how to fix them

In money, as in life, having a plan is important. Creating a budget, tracking your spending, and cutting expenses are all crucial components of your success. But it doesn't happen in a vacuum. Things come up. We make mistakes. And no matter how hard we try to avoid it, unexpected expenses still have a way of destroying our diligent budgeting efforts.

Seriously, shit happens. When it does, we need a shovel to clean it up – and a feasible plan to fix it. Generally speaking, every problem requires a different solution. So, let's take care of the most dangerous issue first: Emergencies.

When it comes to things going wrong, the biggest threats to our budgets are unexpected emergencies. We're talking about the big things like medical problems, car repairs, losing a job – that kind of stuff. These are emergencies which need to be remedied right away. We can't plan for them, and their sudden appearance can destroy our budget and wreak havoc on our finances for months – or even years – to come.

Keeping expenses low and living below our means definitely helps, but that's not always enough. We need a way to protect our budgets and keep them safe from the inevitable setback. This is where an emergency fund comes in.

Don't know what we're talking about? Let's discuss.

WHAT IS AN EMERGENCY FUND?

So, what is an emergency fund?

Maybe you've heard of it before, or maybe you haven't. Either way, the concept is pretty straightforward: An emergency fund is a special stash of money specifically set aside for emergencies.

Yep, this is money you keep lying around just in case something bad happens (and it always does). It's not for buying tickets to a concert. You don't dip into it for new shoes. You don't use it to pay for a night out, tickets to the big game, or a new piece of jewelry. No, no, no.

This money is for emergencies only. And when you're fighting to get out of debt, an emergency fund is one of the most important tools you have at your disposal.

WHY HAVING AN EMERGENCY FUND IS IMPORTANT

By now you understand that your paycheck is your most important wealth building tool. You also know that a zero-sum budget is the most effective tool for harnessing its power. Since these tools are so important, it makes sense that you'd want to protect them from catastrophes, right? You can with an emergency fund. In the same way insurance policies protect your income and assets, an e-fund protects your budget.

Imagine this: You've devoured this book, created your first budget, began tracking and cutting your spending, and started using all of the other dangerously effective debt destroying techniques you've learned. And it's working. You're bouncing off the walls, ecstatic to finally be zeroing down your debt and moving full speed ahead toward living life on your own terms.

> *"This money is for emergencies only. And when you're fighting to get out of debt, an emergency fund is one of the most important tools you have at your disposal."*

And then...

BAAAAAAAAMMMMMMM!!!!!

The unexpected happens. Something comes along and throws a giant wrench into your well-crafted plans. Maybe your car breaks down, or you get sick and miss work, or your water heater takes a dump. Who knows what it is, but something costly happens that you weren't expecting.

Your budget is melting down all around you. What do you do?

Where do you turn? You need to fix the problem – after all, your health, your car, your hot water... these are actual needs, not stuff you can put off.

But, now you need money that you never planned to spend. Where will it come from? Will you be able to handle it, or will you need to go back into debt? Are you going to panic and let it derail all of your hard work?

Blaring Trumpets DUMP DA DA DA!!!!!!

Booming Voice IT'S THE EMERGENCY FUND TO THE RESCUE!

Yep, shit will *definitely* happen. You already know that. So, why not protect your hard work before it inevitably hits the fan?

Emergency funds help smooth the rough patches and pay for emergencies as they arise. Got a flat tire? No problem. Pay for it with your emergency fund. Chip a tooth? Soothe the financial pain by using your emergency fund. Need to miss work for three days because your child is sick? Use your emergency fund to pay the bills this month.

Emergency funds are particularly important when you're first getting started. As you prepare to zero down your debt, unexpected expenses can crush your blossoming financial ambitions. They can blow up your plans and make it extremely difficult to get back on track. And when that happens, it's utterly discouraging. And discouragement leads to failure.

Instead of finding a way through the problem, many people just give up, believing that budgeting can't work for them.

They're wrong.

They *can* do it. They just failed to prepare for the inevitable.

Having an emergency fund helps you avoid this. There's no drama, no unraveling of your plans, no disgusting discouragement. Sure, you may feel a bit disappointed, but you knew something would come up eventually. Instead of getting down on yourself, just dip into your emergency fund, pay for the problem, and keep on truckin', baby! Lickety split, you got this!

But emergency funds aren't just important for zeroing down your debt. It's not like surprise expenses vanish once you're debt-free. To avoid falling back into the cycle of debt you've escaped, you need to keep an emergency fund hanging around then, too.

We've been debt-free for several years, but we still use our emergency fund whenever the need arises. In fact, we recently experienced an expensive string of emergencies that would have derailed our monthly budget – if not for our beautiful e-fund!

First, our furnace went out. Then, the water heater croaked. Of course, the air conditioning unit also busted... right before our lawn mower bit the dust. In total, we racked up about $2,500 in repairs over the course of four months.

Did we worry? Nah. We just used our trusty emergency fund to clean up the mess. We made the repairs, paid for them in cash, and went along our merry way like nothing happened.

That's the beauty of an emergency fund! When you have the money locked and loaded for unexpected expenses, you don't have to worry about what comes next. One little bump in the road (or two... or three) won't destroy your entire financial plan. You won't go spiraling back into the depths of debt and despair. Nope. You just pay it off and move on. You're good to go because you've already prepared for what you knew was coming.

WHAT CONSTITUTES AN EMERGENCY?

Of course, when you're strapped for cash, everything seems like an emergency. It's not. Before you use your e-fund, you want to know that you're facing an actual financial crisis. To determine whether the situation qualifies, ask these three simple questions:

Is the expense unexpected, a surprise, or something you couldn't plan for?

Is the expense necessary?

Can I handle it within this month's budget?

You should *only* use your e-fund for **expenses that you need, couldn't see coming, and can't handle by shifting money around in your current budget**.

For example, suppose you broke your arm. You couldn't plan for that, your copays and deductibles are probably too expensive to handle in your monthly budget, and you need to get it fixed immediately to continue living a normal life. In this instance, using your emergency fund is totally legit. However, you wouldn't want to dip into your emergency fund to pay for a regular checkup. Although necessary, you can plan ahead for it. These types of expenses should be worked into your monthly budget.

Make sense?

Just to be clear, here's a table comparing various emergency expenses with those that should be planned for in your budget.

EMERGENCY FUND EXPENSE	REGULAR BUDGET EXPENSE
• Medical or Dental Emergency • Dead Car Battery • Losing a Job • Broken Window	• Routine Check-Ups • Scheduled Maintenance, Like Oil Changes • Going on Vacation • Remodeling Your Kitchen

As you can see, expenses you can anticipate should be paid with the money available in your monthly budget. For larger items, like a home improvement project or new car, you can even start a separate savings fund specifically marked for those purchases. What you don't want is to start making excuses to use your emergency fund for every little (or large) expense.

WHERE TO KEEP YOUR EMERGENCY FUND

Now that we know when to use our emergency fund, let's talk about where to keep it. Here are two important rules for deciding where to store your e-fund money:

- Your emergency fund should be kept separate from other accounts.

- The money in your emergency fund should be liquid, meaning you can access it immediately.

The money in your emergency fund should be kept separate from your other funds. Why? Because you don't want to mix it up with money you need for other things. It keeps the money in your e-fund safe and separate from your other bills, curbing temptation to spend it on non-emergencies.

When emergency fund money is lumped into the general savings pile, it doesn't feel special. It's just there, hanging out with all of our other Benjamins. Because it doesn't feel special, it's easier to spend... and we don't want that. We need to be sure that we *only* use that money for emergencies. It's got to be used very consciously, and we must be very aware of the circumstances before deciding to spend it. That's why it's important to keep your emergency fund separate from your regular savings.

Still, we don't want to make it too hard to access either. We must be able to reach the money if we really need it. Therefore, our emergency fund should be kept in accounts that are liquid, which means easily and immediately accessible.

"Wait a minute? So, my emergency fund should be hard to get to but easy to access?"

Yeah. Pretty much.

If you keep your emergency fund in a savings vehicle that isn't liquid, you're less likely to use it when you actually need it. For instance, some people may be tempted to stash their emergency cash in an investment or interest-bearing account. After all, it's harder to access AND they'll make money off of their own money. It's an easy mistake to make.

Look, we're all about making your money work for you. We love it when our money makes money, but it's important to keep our goal in mind.

The purpose of this fund is to help you handle emergencies, not to generate income. Withdrawing money from investment accounts usually comes with a catch. By putting your emergency fund into a certificate of deposit, Roth IRA, or a similar account, you're less likely to use the fund for its intended purpose. Instead of using your e-fund to pay for an emergency expense (and taking a hit from early withdrawal fees, taxes, or simple inconvenience), you're much more likely to use debt to stem the tide. That's exactly what we're trying to avoid in the first place!

Do yourself a favor. Keep your e-fund separate but liquid. OK?

So, if keeping your emergency fund in an investment account isn't optimal, where should you keep it? Personally, we'd recommend these three types of savings vehicles for your e-fund:

- Savings account
- Checking account
- Cash

Yup. Just open a free savings or checking account and dump the money in there. That way it's kept separate from your other money, but you still need to make a conscious decision before spending it. Plus, it's easy to access when an emergency arises.

If you want, you can even stick cash under your mattress. Make it harder to access by locking it up in a safe. Heck, you can even put it in a plastic bag and freeze it in a block of ice. You'll have to wait until the ice melts before you can physically access the money, which gives you some extra time to think about the expense before spending it.

Again, we're usually all in favor of getting the best rate of return on your money. That's not the case with emergency funds. Remember that an emergency fund's purpose is to protect your budget by handling emergencies. It may not generate income, but – by safeguarding your budget – it can help make you rich.

HOW TO PREPARE YOUR OWN EMERGENCY FUND

Now, let's talk about how to start an emergency fund of your own.

First, decide where you're going to keep your e-fund using one of the three options we recommended above – savings account, checking account, or cash. Don't spend too much time thinking about this. It probably won't matter which option you choose as long as you pick one and go with it. Action trumps inaction, and the only way out of this debt mess is to move forward.

Next, start saving money in the fund. How much? **Begin by saving a few hundred dollars at a time – or whatever you can afford – until your e-fund is sufficiently stocked.** This shouldn't overburden your budget, but it will give you a good start.

Add your e-fund contributions to your zero-sum budget every month so you can begin saving immediately. List your emergency fund savings along with your regular bills like your mortgage, electric bill, and groceries. Then, fund that baby every month until it's adequately stocked for your lifestyle and needs. Here are some benchmarks to shoot for:

BEGINNER EMERGENCY FUND

Remember, Truth #1 states, "Debt is the single biggest obstacle standing between you and the life of your dreams." To seize control of your money and your life, you must eliminate debt as quickly as possible.

Buuuuuut... you still need to protect your budget. You need a beginner emergency fund.

Until you've worked your way out of debt, you should build a beginner emergency fund of $1,000. So, start saving a few hundred dollars of your take-home pay each month until you've reached that mark.

For some of you, this may seem like a tall order – especially if you've never been great at saving. Don't worry. You already know how to do this. Use the money you're saving by cutting expenses, and stash that money in your emergency fund. Keep putting away money until you have a thousand bucks. Once you do, it's time to destroy your debt! (We'll teach you how to pay off your debt at warp speed in the next chapter.)

FULLY-STOCKED EMERGENCY FUND

Since this book is about zeroing down your debt, we don't want to spend too much time here. But, let's talk briefly about what a fully-stocked emergency fund looks like. Once you've destroyed your debt and worked your way down to zero, you'll have more money to work with. When you do, it's time to build a fully-stocked emergency fund.

Your ultimate aim is to keep three to six months' worth of living expenses stashed away in your emergency fund – enough to cover your mortgage, utility bills, and other essentials. Exactly how much you need depends on your individual situation and how comfortable you are with the size of your cushion. Your monthly expenses, employment situation, and personal need for stability will all factor into this decision. In essence, a fully-stocked e-fund should give you plenty of time to find a new job or right your financial ship if a complete financial meltdown strikes.

As self-employed individuals, we like to err on the conservative side. Because our income is never guaranteed, we typically keep about six to nine months' of expenses in our e-fund.

> *"Although you don't know exactly what's coming, you know it's out there. Get your emergency fund in place right away, and rest easy knowing you can handle whatever comes your way."*

Personally, we would rather be prepared than caught off guard.

Again, we don't want you to worry about fully stocking your emergency fund right at the moment. Just focus on building your beginner emergency fund of $1,000. Get started now.

WHAT TO DO WHEN YOUR EMERGENCY FUND IS DEPLETED

OK. So, you've got a beginner emergency fund loaded with $1,000 (or a fully-stocked emergency fund with three to six months of expenses). Unfortunately, your roof started spewing water onto your bed, so the leak needed to be fixed right away. The good news is that you've tapped into your e-fund to pay for the repairs, and your budget is still sound.

Now what?

It's time to replenish that emergency fund!

To do that, just repeat the steps you used to fund it originally. Save as much as you can each month until the fund is full again. Then, resume your normal budgeting routine, and get back to living your life.

You see, when you have an emergency fund in place, you don't have to worry about every little hiccup. You've already got it covered because you're prepared. Although you don't know exactly what's coming, you know it's out there. Get your emergency fund in place right away, and rest easy knowing you can handle whatever comes your way.

SURVIVING OTHER (SMALLER) BUDGET MELTDOWNS

As we mentioned in the last chapter, the journey to debt freedom is different for everybody, but many of the problems we face are the same. Anybody who's kept a budget for long enough has experienced similar issues and made many of the same mistakes. The way you deal with them can mean the difference between success and failure.

Here are five common budgeting issues and how you can fix them:

Small, Unexpected Expenses: Sometimes, small expenses pop up when we're not expecting them. They aren't emergencies, but you didn't expect or budget for them either. Maybe your child needs money for a field trip, or you locked your keys in your car. To keep from busting your budget, use the money you set aside in your budget's "miscellaneous" category. If you don't have enough, transfer money from one of your other dtscretionary categories to cover the issue. If you find that you're short for small expenses on a regular basis, you may need to budget more for miscellaneous expenses.

Forgetting to Budget for Expenses: Using a monthly zero-sum budget is a great way to keep track of your monthly expenses, but sometimes we forget to account for everything. Maybe it's a bill that's only paid every few months, or maybe it's an event we forgot about. Regardless, don't panic... and don't let it bust your budget. Again, try to fund the expense using money from the miscellaneous category. If you need more, rebalance your budget by using money from other categories to handle the expense. Spend less on entertainment this month, try to save on groceries, or skip the shopping trip you had planned. Just make sure your budget balances to zero when you're finished.

Underestimating Variable Expenses: Estimating your variable expenses can be tricky. After all, they change every month. Budgeting $100 too low on your electric bill can cause a major problem. If this happens, try and shift money around from other categories to pay for the overage. As a last resort, dip into your savings to help cover the costs. Whatever you do, don't take out a loan or put it on credit! In the future, use past bills as an indicator of what you might owe each month. If possible, base your estimate on your bill from the same month last year. Be as accurate as possible, and try overestimating your costs next time around.

Over-budgeting: This is something we all do from time to time, and while it's usually a good problem to have, it can be detrimental. If you have money left over in a certain category at month's end, resist the temptation to spend it. Instead, move it to your e-fund, chuck it at your debt, or use it to fund other savings goals... in that order! Should you find yourself consistently over-budgeting by a lot, it may be time to reassess your estimates. You don't want to underestimate your expenses and come up short, but you don't want to overestimate by so much that you're feeling unnecessarily strapped, either. Use your expense tracking worksheets and past bills as a guide to be as accurate as possible.

Splurge Spending: Let's be honest: No matter how much we plan, no matter how disciplined we are, no matter our good intentions... sometimes we just blow it. We know what we're doing is bad for us, but we do it anyway. It's OK. We're human. Fix the immediate problem by shifting money from other categories to cover the splurge. Then, recommit to diligently executing your budget and get back on track. Don't let one slip-up destroy your entire plan. Better yet, budget the occasional splurge into your monthly plan. Budget for small rewards and treats that will help keep you satisfied and feeling rejuvenated. Just to be clear, we're talking about small items, like $20 or less. These small rewards can help you avoid the gigantic splurge spending that can really destroy your progress.

WRAPPING UP

Remember, things happen. Big, small, in-between – there are always going to be issues that pop up, threatening to destroy your budget. Prepare for them where you can through accurate budgeting and an appropriately stocked emergency fund. If a wound is self-inflicted, do your best to mitigate the problem. Seek out the source and make corrections as needed.

Above all else, be kind to yourself. This is a marathon, not a sprint, and even the best budgeters make mistakes. Just pick yourself up, dust off, and get back on track. The more you practice, the better you'll get. You can do it! We believe in you! Just keep going. When you're reaping the rewards of being debt-free, you'll be grateful you did.

ACTION ITEMS

Decide what savings vehicle you'll use to hold your emergency fund. Don't spend too much time thinking about it. Just pick one and get started... like, now!

Start building a beginner emergency fund. Save at least a few hundred dollars each month until you have saved $1,000.

After you've zeroed down your debt, it's time to fully stock your emergency fund. Save three to six months of expenses in your emergency fund, and sleep well knowing that you can handle almost any financial monkey wrench thrown your way.

NOTES

_____

_____

_____

_____

_____

_____

_____

_____

_____

_____

_____

_____

NOTES

NOTES

NOTES

_____

_____

_____

_____

_____

_____

_____

_____

_____

_____

_____

CHAPTER 7

*Two Dangerously Effective Methods
for Destroying Debt Fast*

In this chapter, you'll learn:

- The 9-Step Process for Achieving Debt Freedom

- One simple tactic required to destroy debt fast

- How to prioritize your debt repayment

- Two dangerously effective methods to zero down your debt once and for all

- Tips and tricks for surviving your debt repayment process

We hope you're as excited as we are! You've learned the fundamentals of good money management. You're rocking a zero-sum budget and cutting your expenses. You've stocked your beginner emergency fund. You have all the tools you need to seize control of your money and your life.

> *"No matter the size of your debt, no matter how deep the hole, you can get out. It is possible. Thousands of people have done it already, and you can too. You just need a strategy. You need a plan."*

Now, it's time to go on the offensive. It's time to zero down your debt... for good!

Remember, your paycheck is the key to building real wealth – and debt is its sworn enemy. Think of your debt like a cancer. It is constantly growing, spreading, and choking the life out of your finances. Just like cancer, you need to get rid of it... and you need to do it fast.

No matter the size of your debt, no matter how deep the hole, you can get out. It *is* possible. Thousands of people have done it already, and you can too. You just need a strategy. You need a plan.

BEHOLD! We give you the 9-Step Process for Achieving Debt Freedom!

NINE STEPS TO DEBT FREEDOM

- Create a zero-sum budget.

- Track your spending and cut unnecessary expenses.

- Temporarily pause your savings goals (retirement savings, college savings, etc.).

- Build a beginner emergency fund.

- Select and use a debt repayment method to zero down your non-mortgage debt.

- Fully stock your emergency fund.

- Resume saving for retirement and other savings goals.

- Pay off your mortgage.

- Enjoy living debt-free!

Every big task is completed by taking small steps. Zeroing down your debt is no different. By prioritizing it into an easy-to-follow process, the scope of the problem becomes a lot easier to digest. Heck, you've already got the first four steps covered!

Here's a quick review:

Create a zero-sum budget: As you know, your zero-sum budget provides the solid foundation on which your entire financial plan is based. Your budget is the most effective tool for harnessing the power of your paycheck. It tells your money where to go, what to do, and how to do it. Your zero-sum budget helps you use the money you already have more efficiently, and that's the most important part of zeroing down your debt.

Track your spending and cut unnecessary expenses: Tracking your spending helps you stay on budget and control your expenses so you can live within (and below) your means. Cutting unnecessary expenses releases money trapped by budget vampires, allowing you to unleash the powerful potential of your paycheck. Below, we'll teach you the specific steps for using that money to zero down your debt at warp speed.

Temporarily pause your savings goals: If you're already saving money toward long-term goals, that's great – but it's time to tap the brakes. Once you've created a beginner emergency fund of $1,000, pause your other savings goals until your debt is paid off. The interest you're making in a savings account is far less than what it's costing you to carry debt. Essentially, you're borrowing money to save. This includes pausing contributions to your 401(k) above the minimum required to earn the employer match. (Note: Only do this if you're fully committed to paying off debt at warp speed!)

You're prepared. You're ready. So let's move on to some specific, step-by-step repayment strategies.

THE SIMPLE TACTIC REQUIRED TO DEFEAT DEBT FAST

We firmly believe that the faster you destroy your debt, the better off you'll be. You want this cancer gone. If taking control of your life doesn't motivate you to zero down your debt quickly – like at *freakin' warp speed* – we don't know what will!

Our goal is to eliminate this debt in a matter of months, not years. Doing so takes a proven, focused, strategic attack. As such, we recommend two extremely effective methods to zero down your debt at warp speed. They are:

The Debt Snowball Method, or **The Debt Avalanche Method**

Both are equally effective and simple. The only difference is the order in which you prioritize your payments. Most importantly, they both center around one simple tactic:

TO GET OUT OF DEBT FAST, YOU MUST PAY MORE THAN THE MINIMUM DUE.

Duh – that seems obvious, right? So, why don't we all do it?

Seriously, making minimum payments is weak. Destroying your debt through extra-large payments? *Now* you're coming strong, player!

Of course, zeroing down your debt at warp speed is more complicated than that. We can't go into this all will-nilly. We can't just throw darts in the dark. Hellllll no! We need to focus.

When faced with multiple issues, it's easy to feel overwhelmed. It's hard to handle numerous problems when your focus is divided. However, breaking things into smaller, manageable chunks relieves stress and usually produces better results.

- The most effective way to tackle multiple tasks is by focusing your energy on completing one task at a time. That's what these methods do. They provide a strategic plan for destroying your debt fast... one at a time. They focus your energy (and your money) so you can zero down your debt in small, bite-sized chunks. Doing so provides fast, trackable results that help you stay motivated to push through the pain and zero down your debt at warp speed.

It's time to get out of debt, and it's time to do it NOW! You're going to take everything you possibly can, every last penny available, and throw it at your debt... *AND*, you're going to do it strategically, keeping the end-goal in mind. Your're going to zero down our debt, FAST, and you're going to take back control of your life.

You can do it. Here's how.

TWO DANGEROUSLY EFFECTIVE METHODS FOR DESTROYING YOUR DEBT AT WARP SPEED

Either of these methods can be equally effective, and they both follow a very similar structure. Although they are designed to pay off debt at extremely quickly, bear in mind that these methods work for paying off debt at any speed. If you want to take it a little slower, follow the same steps outlined below. (In this case, you may not want to pause your retirement savings.) The faster you zero down debt, the better off you'll be... and the more likely you are to power through the tough times and succeed. Choose the one you like best and hop to it!

THE DEBT SNOWBALL METHOD

The "Debt Snowball" method is a big debt repayment strategy that starts off small. With the Debt Snowball, you'll repay your debts one by one, from the smallest balance to the largest. Starting small helps you build momentum and stay emotionally invested as you achieve quick wins, knocking off one debt, and then another and another.

Critics argue the Debt Snowball isn't the best mathematical solution because it doesn't prioritize high-interest debt.

Proponents say the best solution is the one that works, and the Debt Snowball helps build your confidence and commitment. (Besides, if you destroy your debt at warp speed, the difference in interest is relatively negligible.) In any case, the Debt Snowball is the preferred debt repayment method of several popular personal finance personalities and has helped thousands of people defeat their debt.

Here's how to use it:

Step 1: Rank your individual debts by the amount owed, from your smallest balance to the largest. Don't worry about the interest rates or the original loan amounts – pay attention only to your existing outstanding balances. Smaller debts often include individual credit cards, department store cards, personal loans, and other financing arrangements, but that isn't always the case. (Note: At this stage, we're focused on non-mortgage debt.)

Step 2: If that list of debts feels overwhelming, take a deep breath and try to relax. Using the Debt Snowball, you'll start destroying these debts one small chunk at a time. So, take a minute to focus... and get ready to go.

Step 3: Make minimum payments on all of your debts EXCEPT the one with the smallest balance. That's the debt we're going to attack first.

Step 4: Over the course of this book, we've talked about using your budget and expense tracker to cut your expenses. Now, it's time to put that extra cash to work. After you've budgeted for your basic necessities and the minimum payments on your other debts, *use every last remaining dollar to pay extra toward your smallest debt.* Take the money you've saved by cutting cable TV, eating in, and suspending your golf game and throw it as hard as you can at the smallest debt. Pay that sucker off as quickly as possible! Keep repeating this process every month until the smallest debt is paid off in full.

Step 5: Congratulations! You've just paid off your smallest debt. Pat yourself on the back and keep going! Take all the money you were paying toward the debt you just destroyed, and chuck it at the next smallest debt – on top of the minimum payment you were already making! Like a snowball rolling down a hill, your payments will get progressively larger as you move from one debt to the next. Eventually, you'll be making huge payments toward your largest debts, knocking them out in no time. Keep repeating this process until you have everything paid off!

Here's an example of the Debt Snowball in action. Let's say you have four outstanding debts. Ranked from smallest to largest, they are:

Debt 1: $1,000 credit card ($25 minimum payment)

Debt 2: $5,000 credit card ($100 minimum payment)

Debt 3: $10,000 car loan ($250 minimum payment)

Debt 4: $20,000 student loan ($300 minimum payment)

Now, suppose you've cut some expenses and have $1,000 budgeted for debt repayment each month. In this example, you'll make minimum payments on Debts 2, 3, and 4, leaving with you $350 a month to throw at Debt 1 ($1,000-100-250-300=$350).

After three months, Debt 1 will be paid off completely. Then, add the $350 a month to the $100 minimum payment you've been making on Debt 2, for a total of $450 a month. Feel the momentum building? At that rate, Debt 2 will be blasted away in 11 months – at which point you can pile that extra $450 a month on top of your $250 minimum car payment. Look out, auto loan; you'll be toast in about nine more months!

The Debt Snowball method is a great way to score some quick victories in what can be a dispiriting process, keeping you emotionally charged while paying off individual debts in rapid succession.

To get the most out of this strategy, commit to destroying your debt at warp speed! We're talking 24 to 36 months or less. This might mean making radical changes to your lifestyle for a short period of time, like eliminating all unnecessary expenses and living on a "bare bones" budget. The more radical the changes, the faster and more radical your results will be. Remember, these cuts are temporary, but debt freedom could last forever.

THE DEBT AVALANCHE

So, if the Debt Snowball isn't mathematically correct, what is? It's the Debt Avalanche.

The Debt Avalanche method uses practically the same process as the Debt Snowball, with one big exception: Rather than paying off the smallest balances first, you'll prioritize debts according to their interest rate.

Here's how it works:

Step 1: Instead of ordering your debts by the amount owed, this time, arrange them by interest rate. Starting with the highest interest rate first, rank your debts – individually – from the highest to lowest rate. Generally speaking, you'll likely begin by paying off individual credit cards or personal loans, since they usually carry a higher rate than most other debts. At the bottom of the pack, you'll typically find things like auto loans and student loans.

Step 2: Take a moment to focus and relax.

Step 3: Make minimum payments on all of your debts EXCEPT for the bill with the highest interest rate. We'll attack that first.

Step 4: Bust out your budget and expense tracking sheets. Use all of your available discretionary income, including the money you've freed up by cutting your expenses, to make extra payments toward the balance with the highest interest rate.

Step 5: Hammer away at the bill with the highest interest rate every month until it's paid off. Then, take the money you were paying toward that debt and use it to pay the bill with the next highest interest rate (in addition to the minimum payment you were already making).

Step 6: Keep on going until all of your debts are paid off!

Like the Debt Snowball, the Debt Avalanche is a great way to crush your debt fast. Again, this method is geared toward paying off your debt as quickly and *efficiently* as possible. It isn't concerned with getting emotional wins, but it will help you pay less interest overall. If your balance with the highest rate is a big one, it may take a while to crush that first debt. Still, you'll save money by eliminating your high-interest debt first.

So, how do you decide which method is right for you? Those who need an emotional boost to stay motivated might have more luck with the Debt Snowball. If the thought of paying higher interest rates eats you up inside, use the Debt Avalanche. In either case, by committing to the process, you'll see your balances drop like a rock... and keep dropping. And that's always encouraging. Both methods work great, so just choose one and move on.

Tips and Tricks for Surviving the Process

Make no bones about it: Paying off your debt won't be easy. We like to think of it as the hardest simple thing you'll ever do. The steps aren't complicated, but executing them can be extraordinarily difficult.

There will be times when you want to give up. You'll find yourself wondering if it's all worth it. That's OK. Take a deep breath and remember that this process is really a gift to yourself. Gather your senses for a moment, refocus, and push forward. It took you a long time to dig that debt crater. Now, it's going to take time and commitment to get out of it.

Repaying your debt at warp speed requires focus. You'll need to make small but difficult choices. By letting go of your wants for a short time, you'll be free to chase your dreams for the rest of your life.

Here are a few tips to help keep you focused on destroying your debt and taking control of your life:

Consider using your savings to pay off debt. If you have a pile of cash sitting in a savings or checking account, consider using it as a down payment on your debt. You're upside-down.

You've essentially borrowed money to save those funds, and the interest rate you're paying on your debt is likely far higher than what you're earning at the bank. Use your cash to make a quick dent in your debt, and score some instant wins by doing it!

> *"Remind yourself that it will get better. Zeroing down debt at warp speed means making some lifestyle changes. The more radical the change, the quicker you'll see results. Remember that it will get better."*

(Note: **DO NOT** use your emergency fund or retirement plans to do this!)

Use windfalls to your advantage. A few times a year, you might receive some extra money you weren't expecting – like a tax refund, a year-end bonus, or yard-sale earnings. Take that glob of "windfall" money and immediately put it toward your debt. By treating these windfalls as free money and using them wisely, you can eliminate big chunks of debt in one fell swoop.

Cut up your cards. Still tempted to use debt as a cushion? Help yourself out by cutting up all of your credit cards. You're putting a lot of work into reviving your financial life. Why allow yourself to be tempted by easy and available credit? Cut up those cards and avoid debt temptation so you don't sabotage your progress.

Attack your debt without mercy. Debt is destroying your chance to live life on your own terms. Treat it like the cancer it is, and attack it ferociously! Have no mercy. It's certainly showing you none.

Stay positive. The road to debt destruction may seem like a grind, but it's important that you stay the course. That's easier to do with a positive attitude. Even when it seems like you can't make it any further, positivity can carry you through. You can do this! Thousands of people have walked this path before you. They made it and so will you.

Remind yourself that it will get better. Zeroing down debt at warp speed means making some lifestyle changes. The more radical the change, the quicker you'll see results. Remember that *it will get better*. The laser-like focus, the bare-bones budget, your mountain of debt – all of it is only temporary. It will end, and it will get better. Once you've pushed through the fleeting, temporary pain, you'll reap the benefits of these enormous changes for the rest of your life. What's 12, 24, or 36 months of focused debt destruction compared to a lifetime of living debt-free?

Be kind to yourself. You're not the first person to struggle with debt, nor will you be the last. Resist the temptation to beat yourself up. (We'll teach you how in Chapter 9.) Stay positive and be kind to yourself.

Reward yourself. Anybody locked in a bitter battle needs a little down time. Give yourself a break, and enjoy a reward now and then. Just paid off a credit card? Grab a bowl of ice cream to celebrate! Knocked out your student loan? Enjoy a day at the movies. Take your mind off of the fight for a moment, then jump back into the battle. Once you're rested, you'll be ready fight even harder!

WRAPPING UP

Right now, your debt is standing between you and the life you've always dreamed of living. If you want to live life on your own terms, if you want the chance to chase your dreams, if you want to crush the feelings of stress and fear that come from living paycheck to paycheck... it's time to zero down your debt for good.

Attack your debt with courage and tenacity. Destroy it before it destroys you. Once you do, the possibilities are endless.

ACTION ITEMS

Here's what you need to do now:

- Choose one of the dangerously effective methods for debt destruction, either the Debt Snowball or Debt Avalanche. They're both equally effective and similar in practice. Pick one and go with it.

- Order your debts according to your plan. Then, throw every extra penny you can toward repaying your debts, one balance at a time.

- Keep following your debt repayment plan, knocking out one debt after another, until you've destroyed all of your non-mortgage debt.

- Give yourself a pat on the back! You've just zeroed down your debt!

- Keep reading, because you're not done quite yet.

NOTES

NOTES

_____

_____

_____

_____

_____

_____

_____

_____

_____

_____

_____

NOTES

_____

_____

_____

_____

_____

_____

_____

_____

_____

_____

_____

_____

NOTES

_____

_____

_____

_____

_____

_____

_____

_____

_____

_____

_____

In this chapter you'll learn:

- How side hustles can help you pay off debt faster

- Common stalling techniques to identify and avoid

- Different types of side hustles you can start immediately

- How to use your side hustle income to make the biggest impact on your debt

Just for a moment, let's go back to the beginning and look at the first three Fundamental Truths of Destroying Debt and Building Real Wealth:

Truth #1: Debt is the single biggest obstacle standing between you and the life of your dreams.

Truth #2: Your paycheck is your most powerful wealth building tool.

Truth #3: Debt is the enemy of income.

We've spent the majority of this book looking for ways to extend the power of your paycheck, to make the money you already have stretch farther. We've talked about how to manage your money wisely using a zero-sum budget. You've learned to track your expenses and eliminate unnecessary spending. You've discovered that you already have enough money to take control of your life – you just need to use it more efficiently.

But, what if you could find small ways to make *even more money*? Wouldn't that help your debt repayment efforts?

Of course it would. Every little bit helps. But this can only be part of your approach. Don't forget:

Truth #7: Debt neither discriminates nor is cured by income. Rather, it is caused by and controlled through spending.

Before we move forward, it's so important that you understand this: The amount of money you make isn't the problem. Spending is. Trying to cure your debt problem by making more money is akin to putting a Band-Aid on severed artery. You can't solve the problem or expect long-term success by papering over your issues with more money.

We want to be **super** clear about this. Unless you follow the rest of the steps in this book, *you're not going to get out of debt.* You can't just skip ahead to this chapter, start a side hustle, and think everything is going to magically get better because you're earning more! If you don't fix the root cause of your debt – the overspending that got you here in the first place – no amount of side income is going to help your situation.

But, if you work on your spending habits, learn how to create a budget that actually works, and stick to the 10 Fundamental Truths of Destroying Debt and Building Real Wealth, a side hustle can provide exactly the boost you need to get out of debt even faster.

So, let's dig in!

WHAT IS A SIDE HUSTLE?

We freakin' love side hustles! They can be great tools to increase your income, provide you with more options, and help you get out of debt fast. Seriously, we love them.

To get ahead financially, you have to be willing to do things that other people won't. That goes for budgeting. It goes for cutting expenses. It goes for zeroing down your debt. And the same goes for work. It's time to consider a side hustle to boost your success.

Affectionately called side gigs, side jobs, or any number of other terms, side hustles are exactly what they sound like – additional work you take on, beyond the scope of your day job, to earn extra income. That's it.

The monetary benefits of a side hustle are obvious, right? The more money you have coming in, the more freedom you have to make wise spending decisions. And, when you're focused on paying off debt, side hustles provide an additional income stream to help you zero down your debt even faster.

But that's not all.

Sure, a side hustle is great for putting extra cash in your pocket, but there's more to it than that. A side hustle is your own little business. It's your baby to love, nurture, and grow. And starting your own business can teach you more about money than any personal finance book or class.

Running a business gives you an appreciation for hustling and hard work. It reinforces the importance of budgeting and cutting expenses. It forces you to learn about the impact of taxes, cash flow, and other issues – all of which improve your financial literacy and build great money management skills that carry over to your personal life.

Beyond that, side hustles present a new outlook on your current job situation. You gain a greater understanding of how companies are run, what a bottom line really means, and why your boss makes certain decisions. In short, the real-world experience of running your own side hustle provides you with a practical business education you can't find in a textbook or lecture hall.

> *"Running a business gives you an appreciation for hustling and hard work. It reinforces the importance of budgeting and cutting expenses. It forces you to learn about the impact of taxes, cash flow, and other issues – all of which improve your financial literacy and build great money management skills that carry over to your personal life. "*

Starting a side gig helps you to stop seeing success as a product of good luck or sheer accident. Your experience teaches you that success is almost always the result of hard work. You understand that luck happens when hard work, preparation, and opportunity all collide. You learn quickly that, in most cases, luck is created. It's a concept most successful people understand, which is why they continue to be lucky. Give almost any successful person a different set of circumstances, and they would succeed all the same.

But there's something even more important than all that. Something you wouldn't think about unless it has happened to you. Something so huge that it can change your life forever: A side hustle is yours.

It is **yours.**

It's yours to do whatever you wish with it, and its potential is only limited by the size of your market and your willingness to work. Frankly, until you've done it, you may not understand how big of a deal this actually is.

You see, when you work for somebody else, everything is limited:

Limited Income: Your income is limited by the amount of money your employer is willing to pay you. You *might* get small raise or a bonus each year, but you'll only make as much as they are willing to give. Entrepreneurs have uncapped income potential.

Limited Upward Mobility: Your upward mobility is limited. No matter the size of your company, there are only so many positions available. In short, you're always going to have a boss. You'll always work for somebody else. Entrepreneurs call their own shots.

Limited Freedom: Your freedom is limited. You're required to be at work each day at a certain time and for a certain number of hours. Entrepreneurs, meanwhile, can typically create their own schedule. They can work whenever they choose, provided the work gets done.

Limited Vacation: Your time off is limited. Most jobs allow for a set amount of days you can request off per calendar year. When you use them, you're done. So, as an adult, you're left to beg and plead with other adults to let you go and do adult things. How is that freedom? Entrepreneurs call their own shots because they get paid for their work, not their time.

When you have a side hustle, you are the boss. Grow your business as large (or as small) as you'd like. Use the extra money to supplement to your regular income. Better yet, grow your new side hustle into your full-time job. That's where the real freedom starts.

Think about it: The wealthiest people in the world are usually business owners, with about half of all millionaires owning their own business. Why is that? Because they know that the most

> *"Thomas Edison said, "Opportunity is missed by most people because it is dressed in overalls and looks like work." In a nutshell, that describes a side hustle. It is your opportunity to succeed."*

valuable thing they have to offer is time. They use their time to create products and services that make money. Then, they pay employees like you to sell or deliver the products, allowing them to focus more time on creating and making more money.

When you work for yourself, you aren't paid for your time. You're paid for what you accomplish. You don't have to punch a clock or beg for time off. Your time is yours to do with as you please. You work to live instead of live to work.

That's what happened to us. We started a financial blog as a way to have fun, keep ourselves accountable, and make a little extra money on the side. We worked our tails off, and as the website grew, so did our side income.

Eventually, we turned writing into our full-time jobs. Now, we make well over six figures a year, are able to travel the world, and enjoy a sense of freedom and security that most people will never experience. It all became possible because we started a side hustle and zeroed down our debt.

Of course, becoming a business owner isn't necessarily the goal. The most important thing you can do now is use any extra money earned from a side hustle to zero down your debt even faster. Because once you're debt-free, the doors of opportunity swing wide open.

WHAT DO YOU NEED TO START A SIDE HUSTLE?

What do you need to start a side hustle? Well, that depends on what you're planning to do. But the most important part of starting a side hustle is found right in the name: You need to HUSTLE.

So, what is hustling? It's going out and finding work that you deserve. It means not being afraid to take risks. It means putting your pride aside and not being scared of the outcome. In short, it means being willing to work harder than you've ever worked before... and then pushing a little more.

Thomas Edison said, "Opportunity is missed by most people because it is dressed in overalls and looks like work." In a nutshell, that describes a side hustle. It is your opportunity to succeed.

There are all kinds of excuses not to start a side hustle. You might be thinking:

- I don't have time. (Yes. You do.)

- I don't have the skills. (Yes. You do.)

- I'll start it when... (Stop procrastinating. Take action now.)

But I don't know anything about business. (You'll learn. Take action.)

Seriously, a side hustle doesn't have to be complicated or complex. Avoid overthinking or overanalyzing the situation – just freakin' do it. You have the same 24 hours in a day as everyone else who's ever started a side hustle or become a success. Don't fool yourself by saying you don't have the time. And, as far as business acumen goes, if you can add 2 + 2, you're good to get started.

Don't worry about every little possibility. It will paralyze you. You can create all the plans in the world, but until you have a product or service that's actually for sale, your plans mean little. Plus, plans always change. Instead of planning your idea to death, take action. Plan, yes... but plan quickly and don't get bogged down in the process.

TYPES OF SIDE HUSTLES

What are you waiting for? It's time to create your own side hustle, like NOW. Here are a few ideas to help you get started. All of these came right off the top of our heads, and it only took about 10 minutes to put together. Here you go:

- Clean houses
- Organize kitchens and closets
- Virtual assistant
- Personal assistant
- Virtual store owner
- Mow lawns
- Rake leaves
- Shovel snow
- Landscaping services
- Hairdresser
- Manicurist
- Personal cuddler (yup, these exist)
- Housesitting
- Babysitting
- Watch pets
- Dog walker
- Start a blog
- Paint houses
- Tax preparation

- Basic elderly care
- Personal shopper
- Freelance writing
- Website designer
- Tutoring
- Wellness coaching
- Handyman
- Freelance mechanic
- Freelance auto body repair
- Newspaper delivery
- School bus driver
- Coach a sport
- Officiate a sport
- Drive for Uber or Lyft
- Take surveys online
- Wait or bus tables
- Clean gutters
- Landlord
- Property manager
- Computer repair
- Teach a course
- Buy and sell rare coins

- Wash and detail cars

- Provide graphic design services

- Be a weekend or wedding DJ

- Deliver pizzas

- Lifeguard

- Collect and sell fishing bait

- Place an ad on your car

- Become a local tour guide

- Plan events

- Sell blood plasma

- Salvage and sell antiques

- Teach a musical instrument

- Sell crafts online or at craft fairs

There are hundreds, heck, thousands more ideas for side hustles out there – not to mention the most basic side hustle of all, getting a part-time job. Get creative. See what you can come up with. What skills do you have that people would be willing to pay for? Do you already own any equipment or tools that you can use? Write down your ideas, choose one or two of them, and get started hustling right away.

HOW TO USE YOUR SIDE HUSTLE INCOME TO GET AHEAD

Alright. You've started your side hustle, and you're starting to rake in a little bit of cash! You've taken action, and you're starting to see results. Congratulations!

So, what next? What do you do with that money?

Why, throw it at your debt, of course!

Go back to your debt repayment plan, and use every penny you make from your side hustle to pay extra toward the debt you're currently focused on. Made $20 mowing lawns? Throw it at your debt. Scraped together $200 driving for Uber? Use it to pay off debt. Picked up $50 for babysitting the neighbor's kids? You got it – chuck it straight at your debt.

Remember, every money decision you make has consequences. Just like every purchase delays your debt freedom, every cent you throw at your debt accelerates the payoff process. The faster you get rid of your debt, the faster you'll be able to enjoy the fruits of your labor. So hop to it!

ACTION ITEMS

Study our list of side hustles or create a list of your own. Choose one or two of them. Then, get to work. Print business cards, knock on doors, post on social media, and hand out flyers to get the word out. Do whatever you need to do to start making some extra money.

Use the money you earn from your side hustle to accelerate your debt repayment plan.

Grow your side hustle into a business. Coddle it, nurture it, and expand it to be as large as you want. Use the money as a supplement to your regular income, or grow it large enough to replace your nine-to-five job.

Pay off your debt... STAT!!!

NOTES

_____

_____

_____

_____

_____

_____

_____

_____

_____

_____

_____

NOTES

NOTES

_____

_____

_____

_____

_____

_____

_____

_____

_____

_____

_____

In this chapter you'll learn:

- The two biggest causes of failure and how to avoid them

- How to develop a strong sense of commitment

- To seize power through controlling your thoughts

- To recognize five "Action Traps" and learn how to avoid them

- How to take positive, concrete steps toward completing your goals

> *"Whether you realize it or not, every second of every day, you're having conversations with yourself. There's a constant stream of words running through your mind, and it shapes the way you think about everything – including money. "*

Throughout this book, we've provided you with practical tools and techniques that will have a huge impact on your financial well-being. Zero-sum budgets, tracking your spending, emergency funds, and debt repayment plans – these are the items that will help you get out of debt and seize control of your life. But for any plan to work, you need to believe in the possibilities. For the best results, you must discard your limiting beliefs and get out of your own way.

Whether you realize it or not, every second of every day, you're having conversations with yourself. There's a constant stream of words running through your mind, and it shapes the way you think about everything – including money. Have you ever heard yourself saying or thinking any one of these things below? Chances are, you've thought or said aloud:

- I'll never get out of debt.

- I'm bad with money.

- I'm not smart enough to be rich.

- Managing money is too complex.

- Money is the root of all evil.

- Money is the solution to all my problems.

- Rich people are horrible.

- Rich people are my heroes.

- My friends and family will leave me if I stop spending money.

- Et cetera, et cetera, et cetera...

These are all limiting beliefs. They limit your ability to survive and thrive. They hold you back from chasing your dreams.

Here's the worst part: **They aren't true.**

Forget everything you think about money. It is all baggage. It's junk, and it's not going to help you zero down your debt. Managing money doesn't take a genius. Money is neither good nor evil. **Money is a tool to help you buy the things you want and need – nothing more.**

TWO MAJOR CAUSES OF FAILURE

Limiting beliefs are actually a self-defense mechanism that we create. In our lifetimes, we take many risks; when they don't work out, we feel pain. Naturally, we're inclined to avoid pain, so we've learned to "protect" ourselves by conjuring up limiting beliefs that frighten us into inaction.

Some of them are helpful, but most of them are not. "Will people think I'm weird? Will my friends and family still like me? Can I even get out of debt?" By "protecting" us, our limiting beliefs keep us from even trying, doing a great deal of damage to the lives we want to live.

So, what are the things we fear most? Why do we fail to take action even when we know it's the right thing to do?

Generally speaking, much of our fear stems from two places:

- The fear of failure.

- The fear of rejection.

FEAR OF FAILURE

In most cases, we don't fail for a lack of knowledge, skill, or talent. *Failure happens because we quit.* Things get too difficult or don't go the way we expect. Sometimes we run out of inspiration or tire from being overworked. Maybe we lose our focus and get distracted. There are a million reasons why, but in the end we quit. Then, we feel like a failure.

It sucks to fail. It feels crappy. But every time we start something and don't finish, it's that much easier to quit the next time around... and the next. By quitting, we teach ourselves that failure is OK – which reinforces our negative self-doubts and increases those crappy feelings of failure. We begin to fear failing itself. So, instead of trying something new, we succumb to the fear of failure instead. If we don't try it to begin with, we can't fail at it. Sound familiar?

Of course, had we just held on a little longer, completed the tasks at hand, piece by piece, we'd finish. Instead of failure, we'd feel a sense of accomplishment. We'd have a positive attitude about starting something new, feeling like there's nothing that could stand in our way.

Finishing what you start isn't some mystical formula known to only the most successful people in our world. It's a skill, and it can be learned. Once you master it, your success continues to feed more and more success. You'll no longer fear failure. You'll be excited by the opportunity to try.

You can do it. Just take small steps, adjust the way you think, and finish what you start.

FEAR OF REJECTION

Look around you. Everywhere you turn, someone wants your money. You're constantly bombarded with advertising and messaging. On top of that, there's a ton of social pressure around spending. Based on absolutely nothing, society has created a gajillion ideas of what is socially acceptable and what isn't. It's the "being cool" concept, and it's costing you dearly.

To be cool, we need to dress a certain way, own the latest gadgets, listen to the right music, and drive the right car. We're afraid we won't fit in if we don't follow the "norms." So we pay a premium to look cool in front of friends, family, and strangers alike.

Businesses love when you compete with the Joneses because it increases their profits. The media wants you to spend because advertisers pay their bills. Politicians encourage spending because it stimulates the economy. Even the Joneses want you to compete, so they can justify their own spending habits.

The whole game is a giant hamster wheel, designed to make you want things you don't need so you'll spend money you may not even have. Worse, it's all based on making you afraid of what others might think. It's a game with no end, and it will keep you from achieving the things you really want in life.

Want to get ahead? *Stop caring what other people think.* They're too busy worrying about themselves to give a shit anyway. And if they do care what you're wearing, driving, or buying, that's their freakin' problem. It's not their money to spend. As the popular saying goes, "Those who matter don't mind, and those who mind don't matter."

Seriously, *stop trying to keep up with the Joneses*. The game is rigged so you'll never win. Somebody is *always* going to have something better, nicer, prettier, or faster than yours. **The only way to win this game is by not playing!**

SQUASHING LIMITING BELIEFS

"Man often becomes what he believes himself to be. If I keep saying to myself that I cannot do a certain thing, it is possible that I may end by really becoming incapable of doing it. On the contrary, if I have the belief that I can do it, I shall surely acquire the capacity to do it even if I may not have it at the beginning."   - Mahatma Gandhi

It sounds silly doesn't it, that you can do anything you put your mind to? Could the human mind possibly be that powerful? "This is just a bunch of New Age psychobabble," you tell yourself.

"It can't help me." Somewhere, deep in the back of your mind, your insecurities are laughing at you.

That's your fear, and it's trying to scare you into submission.

To change the way you live, you need change the way you think. Positive thoughts lead to positive actions... and actions lead to change. In essence, you become what you think about, and you can train yourself how to think.

When you change the way you think about money, your relationship to it changes. You'll let go of your fears and limiting beliefs and start accepting that your dreams really are possible. You understand that you can have everything you've ever wanted, accomplish every goal you've ever set, and realize every dream you didn't even know you dreamt – all by changing the way you think.

How do you train your thoughts to benefit you? Simple. Counter negative thoughts by replacing them with positive ones. Use positive affirmations.

We know, we know. The thought of using positive affirmations seems so lame, so dorky. Repeating positive thoughts makes you feel weird and uncomfortable. What would people think if they actually knew you used positive affirmations?

Who cares?!? That's the fear talking again. Fight through it and just do it.

The reason so many philosophers, motivators, and therapists recommend positive affirmations is because they work. Seriously, try them for 30 days and see if you don't notice a change in the way you think, feel, and act.

Here's your mission: Each time you engage in negative self-talk or repeat a limiting belief, correct it with a positive statement. Jot down all the negative statements you hear in your mind (or coming out of your mouth), and write the correction beside them. Repeat those positive statements 10 times daily until you've quieted the negative voices in your head. Doing so helps you control your thoughts, your debt, and your life.

FINDING YOUR "WHY" AND CREATING A GOAL

Zeroing down your debt isn't easy. There will be times you'll want to give up. You'll think you can't do it, and you'll be tempted to go back to the old cycle of giving up and fearing failure.

- The best way to combat that temptation is to discover your "why." The stronger your motivation to become debt-free, the better chance you'll have to finish.

- Grab a piece of paper and challenge yourself to come up with something that really motivates you, something that will help push and inspire you when times are toughest. Don't just come up with a generic answer like, "I want to be rich." Make it specific. The more specific you are, the stronger your "why" becomes, and the better off you'll be.

- Maybe you want to get out of debt so that you can travel the world. Maybe your "why" is putting your children through college because you couldn't afford it for yourself. Perhaps it's because you need money to help pay for your mother's prescriptions or your child's medical bills. Or, maybe it's something simple, like feeling safe and secure with a roof over your head... and you can't stand the thought of somebody being able to take it away from you.

- Find your "why." Write it down. Keep it safe, and bust it out when you need some motivation.

Now that you have your #1 motivation written down, support it! Come up with more reasons why you want to be debt-free. The more reasons you have to fall back on, the more likely you'll be to follow through.

Using a sheet of paper, write down every reason you can think of. Jot them all down. Challenge yourself to come up with at least 25. Stick this away and use it for extra motivation when you need it.

Now, try one last trick we learned from master motivator Earl Nightingale. Grab another small sheet of paper or an index card.

On it, write the following:

- I will be debt-free in X months.

(Insert your own timeframe for the "X.")

Don't have paper? Type it into the notes section of your smartphone or tablet if you wish. Just write it down. Make it concrete. Send this into the universe as if there is nothing that can stop you from achieving this goal.

Then, read it aloud to yourself several times a day. Do it first thing when you get up in the morning, and read it right before you go to bed. Take it to work and read it quietly to yourself. Keep your goal front and center in your mind. Train your thoughts and focus on this goal. When you focus your thoughts on obtaining exactly what you want, you'll be spurred on to take steps toward achieving it. Make this a habit for 30 days, and you will see results.

TIPS FOR CREATING POWERFUL POSITIVE AFFIRMATIONS

The more powerful your positive statements are, the bigger impact they'll have on how you think. Here are a few tips:

- **Use Positive Statements**: Positive statements are more effective than negative ones. For instance, rather than saying "I don't want to be broke," change the phrasing to "I will be wealthy."

- **Be Specific**: Be as specific as possible. "I will be worth $1 million dollars by age 55," is more powerful than "I will be rich."

- **Assume Success**: Use powerful words to describe your goals, and always assume success. Instead of "I wish I could travel more," or "I'd like to go to Italy," try "I will travel to Rome by age 33." Frame your statement as if there is no way you can fail.

- **Give Your Goal a Timeline**: Without a clear timeframe

for accomplishing goals, it's easy to put them off until later. Creating a timeline for your goals motivates you to take action. It focuses your energy and helps you accomplish your goals more quickly.

TAKING ACTION AND AVOIDING ACTION TRAPS

Most of the time, people don't succeed on talent or their ideas alone. The world is full of big ideas and unrealized potential. Successful people win because they are doers. They don't wait for the right time, don't get caught up in unimportant details, and refuse to ask permission to be awesome. Successful people take action.

All of the planning, preparation, and positive thinking in the world won't matter unless you take action. You need to go out and get what you want, and know that you deserve every last bit of it. That means avoiding the following "Action Traps" which can zap your momentum. Here's how to identify these pitfalls – and how to avoid or power through them.

Action Trap #1: Over-Planning

Many of us love to plan for every possible contingency. We tell ourselves that we have to be ready for anything thrown our way. So, instead of taking action, we plan... and plan... and plan... and plan. We spend all of our energy perfecting a really great plan that never amounts to squat because we don't take action.

Stop. Realize when enough is enough. Have a clear and specific idea of what you want to accomplish, start with the end goal in mind, but be flexible with how you're going to get there. No matter how much you plan, those plans must change and adapt as you move along. Stop planning and start moving. Your plans will never allow you to reach your dreams. Only your actions will.

Action Trap #2: Getting Lost in the Details

In some ways, being detail-oriented is a great thing. Typically, if you take care of the small details, big picture items fall into place.

But, you need to focus on the *right* details. If not, you'll stunt your progress by getting lost in things that are unimportant.

A concept that is 90% perfect and sent into the world is immeasurably better than one that's 100% perfect and stuck in your head. Let go of the idea of perfection. Instead, take action. Action trumps inaction (almost) every time.

Action Trap #3: Waiting for the Perfect Time

There's a persistent myth that we must wait for the perfect time before starting something new. We "can't" date because we're too focused on school, can't get married because of our career, or can't travel because of the kids. We'll start saving for retirement once the car is paid off, or once we turn 30... or 35... or 40. Instead of taking action on our dreams, we put them off until later – until the "right time."

News flash: There is NEVER a right time. Something always comes up. The "right time" is just an excuse, delaying us from taking action now. It helps us avoid making changes that scare us. Stop telling yourself that it's not the right time, and see this for what it really is: A stalling tactic that is usurping your happiness, suspending your goals, and delaying your dreams. There is no right time, except for right now!

Action Trap #4: Asking for Permission

Most of us drift through life, playing by rules designed to keep us afraid and in line. We're conditioned to ask for permission. We constantly ask ourselves questions like, "Is this OK?" and "I wonder if they'll let me do that?" Rather than controlling our own destiny, we ask permission to live.

When you control your money, you don't need to ask permission. Everything you want is within your grasp. Stop asking for permission and start doing something! Seize control of your finances. Take action now.

Action Trap #5: Giving In to Fear

When it comes down to it, every action trap revolves around fear. But, what's the worst that can happen? You'll get out of debt and take that family trip to China you've always dreamed about? Somebody might think you're strange because you live life on your own terms? You could fail, pick up the pieces, and learn from your mistakes?

Plato said, "Courage is knowing what not to fear." Stop being afraid. Stop caring what other people think! Your fear is fabricated. It's in your head. This is *your* life – your one and only shot to get this right! Be brave and put yourself out there. The world rewards those who are brave enough to ask and take action. Don't wait until tomorrow. Start living the life you've always dreamed of today!

WRAPPING UP

"Learn to enjoy every minute of your life. Be happy now. Don't wait for something outside yourself to make you happy in the future. Think how really precious is the time you have to spend, whether it's at work or with your family. Every minute should be enjoyed and savored." – Earl Nightingale

Be brave. Have courage. Know that you will accomplish everything that you *truly* set your mind to. You have the power to destroy your debt and live life on your own terms. It's all there inside of you. All you have to do is reach out and grab it!

ACTION ITEMS

On a piece of paper, jot down your limiting beliefs and negative self-talk. Correct each item with positive affirmations. Repeat these positive statements 10 times each day until you eliminate your resistance to self-love.

Grab an index card and write this down: I will be debt-free in X months. (Insert your own timeframe in place of the X.) Bust out your card, and repeat this goal aloud to yourself first thing in the morning, last thing at night, and several times throughout the day. Keep your goal front and center, and focus your thoughts on it.

Create a list of 25 reasons why you want to become debt-free. If at any time you're feeling discouraged throughout your journey, bust out this list and use it for motivation. Remind yourself why you started this process in the first place.

Beware of any action traps that may be holding you back from getting started. Identify them and power through.

NOTES

NOTES

_____

_____

_____

_____

_____

_____

_____

_____

_____

_____

_____

NOTES

NOTES

_____

_____

_____

_____

_____

_____

_____

_____

_____

_____

_____

In this chapter, you'll learn:

- How it feels to become debt-free

- Where to focus your energy once you've paid off your non-mortgage debt

- How to complete the 9-Step Process for Achieving Debt Freedom

- The basics of saving for retirement and college

- Why paying off your mortgage early may be right for you

- How to give generously without injuring your own goals

YEEEEEESSSSSSS!!!!!!

Congratulations! You've worked hard, zeroed down your non-mortgage debt, and are debt-free except for your house!

It must feel freakin' fabulous right?!

We'll tell you this: It does... and it doesn't.

It's an incredible feeling to zero down your debt. You've been so focused for such a long time, and it feels amazing to accomplish one of the most important goals you'll ever set. The initial rush of excitement and sense of accomplishment will last... a few days at most. Then, it's back to normal life.

When we became debt-free, it was incredibly exhilarating to write that last check. We'd worked so hard to make our debt-free dreams come true, and we were proud of what we'd accomplished. With that final signature, we felt like the band should strike up a tune while streamers and confetti fell from our ceiling.

Yeah, that didn't happen.

Nobody could have cared less... except for us, of course. When we told others, they replied with an uncomfortable, "Oh, that's nice," and promptly changed the subject. After all the effort and sacrifice required to finally hit zero, the moment it actually happened almost felt like a let-down.

Crazy, right?

We've spent this whole book pumping you up, telling you how awesome it is to become debt-free, only to tell you at the end that it's a let-down?!? WTF, right?!?

Trust us. The reward is there.

Sure, there may not be any celebrations, marching bands, or TV reporters clamoring to hear your story – but your reward is waiting. Just like everything else you've done in this book, your reward is a long-term one. It isn't a delicious cup of instant gratification to suck down and enjoy immediately. It takes time for your amazing accomplishment – and its rewards – to sink in.

Once you're debt-free, your paycheck is all yours. So, while your friends sit home drowning in credit card debt, you've got the cash to attend a concert - in London - without going back into debt. As others slave away just to make their car payments, you have the funds to vacation in Aruba… and Jamaica… and the Bahamas… all in a single year. And, while everyone you know will have to keep working into their 60s and 70s, you know you'll be able to retire if you want to… maybe even early.

You've made it. You're debt-free. You have options.

And that is the biggest reward of all.

WHAT'S NEXT?

So, you're debt-free. What's next? You've spent months waging an intense battle requiring incredible amounts of energy and focus. What the heck do you do with all of that?

For starters, let's get back to the process.

Once you've zeroed down your non-mortgage debt, it's time to continue with the 9-Step Process for Achieving Debt Freedom. You remember that right? We talked about it all the way back in Chapter 7. Flip back for a refresher if you need to.

To save you a little time, we'll help you out: You've just completed Step 5.

So, what's next? Steps 6 through 9! That's what!

STEP 6: FULLY STOCK YOUR EMERGENCY FUND

Back in Chapter 6, we talked all about emergency funds. At the time, we asked you to save $1,000 in a beginner emergency fund… and it probably saved your budget at one point or another, didn't it? Cool beans. Now, it's time to protect yourself a little bit more. It's time to fully stock that emergency fund.

As you'll recall, a fully-stocked emergency fund consists of three to six months' worth of expenses. Why is this important? Just because you're out of debt doesn't mean shit stops happening. Stuff comes up, stuff you didn't plan for. And, this *stuff* can completely destroy your budget – or even send you back into debt – if you aren't prepared to handle it.

That's why having a fully-stocked emergency fund is so important. It gives you a cushion to absorb unexpected expenses, even when you're struggling.

Why three to six months of expenses? A cushion this large should help you to continue living life as normal if all hell breaks loose. Let's say your car breaks down, your roof is leaking, and your washing machine takes a crap... all at once. No problem. Just dip into your emergency fund to make the repairs and move on with your life.

Or, maybe you get injured and can't work for a few weeks. Yes, the loss of income still stings; but, with an emergency fund, it won't destroy you. Use your emergency fund to pay your expenses, get healthy, and move on. This is an emergency after all!

Of course, there's also the nuclear bomb of personal finance: You lose your job. Yeah, it's awful. It freakin' hurts, financially and emotionally. But, you don't need to panic. You've got your expenses covered for three to six months, allowing you enough time to find another job.

Remember, emergency funds should be kept separate from your other savings goals. We don't want you dipping into investment accounts or taking on debt to handle emergencies. Your e-fund should be held in an account that is separate but liquid, so you can get to it when needed.

And remember the most important rule: Money from your e-fund should be used *for emergencies only*. Routine maintenance, special events, and other items you can plan ahead for should be included in your budget for that month. Attending a surprise birthday party is not an emergency. Repairing a busted water pipe is.

Keeping an emergency fund is like having your own financial disaster preparedness plan! It's there to help you when times are tough and save you from panicking when emergencies arise. Because, when we panic, we do stupid things with our money. Pump cash into that e-fund until it's fully stocked, and you'll be able to sleep well at night.

STEP 7: RESUME SAVING FOR RETIREMENT AND OTHER SAVINGS GOALS

Once you're out of debt and are protected with a fully-stocked emergency fund, it's time to resume saving for your retirement and other goals. But let's start with retirement. Why? Because when it comes down to it, your other goals can wait.

If needed, kids can pay for their own college educations. You can put off that trip to Europe. Your carpet will be fine for another 12 months. Unfortunately, nobody is going to foot the bill for your retirement except for you. Got it?

As you'll recall, we asked you to pause saving for retirement while you blasted your way through destroying debt. That goes back to the one-thing-at-a-time theory. When your focus is split in too many directions, you don't get anything done... and what you do get done is done poorly. If you want results, you need to focus your energy – and your money – on one thing at a time. Since getting out of debt is going to pay *huuuuuuge* dividends over the long-run, we think it's better for you to hit pause on your retirement goals for a short time.

Again, we want to be very clear here. If you're not going to commit to the system and destroy your debt at warp speed (measured in months, not years), you're doing yourself a disservice by not saving for retirement. But, if you're really serious about paying off your debt quickly and changing your life, not saving for retirement for

12 to 18 months is OK – provided you're using the extra money to pay down your debt faster, of course.

Now that you've worked the program and have all of your non-mortgage debt zeroed down, it's time to resume saving for retirement. But, how much should you save?

Well, that depends.

If your employer offers a retirement plan through work, most experts suggest saving 10% to 15% of your income in the plan. Depending on the type of plan offered, your employer may match around 4% of your income. That gives you an effective retirement savings totaling between 14% and 19% of your income every year. If you're lucky, you may receive a profit-sharing stipend as well. (Note that employers are never required to make those types of contributions, so don't count it in your savings estimates.)

Regardless of how much you decide to save in your work-sponsored retirement account, your bare minimum contribution should be enough to earn the full employer match. So, if the employer match is up to 3% of your income, you need to save no less than 3%. That's **free money** being **offered to you** for **your** retirement. When you're trying to build wealth, there's nothing quite like free money. Take advantage of FREE whenever you can! However, be sure to speak with your investment specialist before making any decisions on what is right for you.

If you're self-employed, saving for retirement is even more imperative. As you well know, saving for your retirement is all on you. There is no employer match, no free money, because *you are* the employer. So, you need to be putting even more money away, and you need to be using the right investment vehicles to do it.

As self-employed individuals, we save at least 20% of our income in retirement accounts. That may seem like a lot, but remember, it's all on us. Somebody's gotta do it!

The cool thing about being self-employed is that you have a number of tax-advantaged retirement savings plans available to you. There are Traditional and Roth IRAs, SIMPLE and SEP IRAs, Individual

401(k) plans, and more. They all have their own rules, contribution limits, and tax advantages, which means this stuff can get pretty complicated. While it's possible to set it up on your own, it may be best to contact a retirement planning specialist for help. No matter where you decide to save for retirement, make sure you're putting money away *somewhere*.

Now that you've got retirement taken care of, it's time to start saving for your other goals. This may mean saving up a down payment for a house, stashing money away for holiday spending, or scraping cash together for a new car.

If you've got kids, this often means saving for college, too. Like many parents, one of our biggest dreams is to help our kids pay for college. And why not? College costs are through the roof, but many "good" jobs require a college education. Besides, we just worked our way out of debt, and we know how it can hold us back. Why would send our kids off to college burdened by a bunch of loans, putting them behind the financial eight-ball before they even graduate? It doesn't make sense, right?

Saving for college is an admirable goal, and it's one that we personally share with you. Each month, we stash away a little bit of money in our daughters' college funds. Additionally, whenever they get birthday money, most of it goes straight toward college savings. At the end of the year, we top it off to claim our state's generous tax break.

College savings plans vary by state, so do some research on 529 plans, UGMA/UTMAs, and Educational Savings Accounts. Learn about the advantages and disadvantages they provide in your area. Then, speak with your investment advisor about what type of plan is right for your situation.

STEP 8: PAY OFF YOUR MORTGAGE

Here's where some of the real fun begins. It's time to pay off your mortgage early!

(GASP!)

> *"Plus, remember that saying about "He who has the gold makes the rules?" When you owe money to someone else, they're in control of your situation. What's more important than being in control of the roof over your head?"*

Yep. We said it. Pay that bizzle off early!

We know it sounds crazy, but bear with us. You can actually own a house, in this country, **without** paying a mortgage. We know *most* people don't do it, but most people never zero down their debt either.

Your house is likely the biggest investment purchase you'll ever make. The thing is, when you finance a house, you don't really own it. The bank does. Plus, that purchase price you agreed to? Yeah... about that. You're paying a bit more than that, aren't you?

You might convince yourself, "By golly, we got a great deal. We only paid $180,000 for this house!" Yeah. You didn't. Depending on your mortgage terms and interest rate, you'll probably pay an extra $50,000 to $150,000 for it. You just won't notice because it gets drained away so slowly.

Of course, you know this already. You know you'll pay more than the purchase price. You know you're paying interest; it just doesn't feel like it's costing you that much. You get used to it, and it lulls you to sleep.

But that's REAL MONEY, yo! That's an extra $50,000 to $150,000 you could have in your pocket if you didn't pay it to the bank.

Plus, remember that saying about "He who has the gold makes the rules?" When you owe money to someone else, they're in control of your situation. What's more important than being in control of the roof over your head?

Look, we know there are people out there who are against paying off your mortgage early. We know all about opportunity cost – that we can use the money for something else. Perhaps we can invest it and make more money on our money. And, mathematically, they may be right.

But this is all about freedom and risk. When the bank owns your house, and that's the reality when you have a mortgage, you are at risk of losing it. It happens all the time. Look no further than the housing crisis of 2007-2009, when millions of Americans lost their homes to foreclosure. Real estate bubbles and predatory lending practices aside, this reminder should be all the motivation you need to pay that sucker off.

When you hear arguments against paying off your mortgage early, it helps to follow the money. Remember who benefits. When you pay off your home loan early, nobody makes a commission. Nobody can sell you a new loan, or a new retirement product, or a new whatever. The bank earns way less money in interest. It doesn't benefit anyone... except for you.

If you need more proof, go ahead and ask someone who's done it. Ask anybody who's paid off their house early if they think it was a mistake. So far, we've never met anyone who does.

Besides, this isn't a zero-sum game. Since you're already debt-free, there's no reason you can't invest AND pay off your house early.

So, start hammering away at your mortgage. Throw extra money toward the principal each month. Destroy that debt just like you did the others! And when you're done, you can live knowing that your house is all yours... and yours alone.

STEP 9: ENJOY LIVING DEBT-FREE

You've made it! You're now *completely* debt-free!

You're free to save. You're free to spend. You're free to give. You are free... and you've earned it.

Without any debts to pay, you can start socking away cash for anything you want. Need new windows? Start saving up. Need a new car? It's time to save. Want to take a trip to the Bahamas? Save. Save. Save. Because your paycheck is no longer spoken for, you'll reach these savings goals in lightning speed.

It's your money. It doesn't belong to anybody else. You can spend it as you please and live life on your own terms. But, don't go backwards. Stick to your budget, and save cash to pay for the things you want. Your paycheck is more powerful than it's ever been before. Don't jeopardize it by falling back into old habits.

A NOTE ON GIVING

A lot of people ask us about giving throughout the entire process. While we admire your generous spirit, it's important not to make that mistake. If you end up giving while you're in debt, you're effectively borrowing money so that you can give it to other people.

You wouldn't take out a loan so you can turn around and give it to charity would you? Well, that's essentially what you're doing when donating while in debt. You're just shifting money around so it doesn't feel that way.

We know you're a generous person. We're right there with you. We think giving is a great and important part of leading a full life. It's a wonderful way to help others while feeding your soul. Giving is a win for everybody, and it is something we whole-heartedly believe in.

But...

Don't give away money you don't have. You can't save others when you're drowning yourself. If giving is important to you, get out of debt fast. Use it as motivation to destroy your debt at warp speed. Then, give all you want. But, before you do, get out of debt.

Give often. Give generously. Give when you're debt-free.

WRAPPING UP

We know this has been a long journey. We know there have been times when you've struggled, when you wanted to give up, when you didn't think you could go any further.

But, you didn't quit.

You made it.

You persevered and you prevailed.

Congratulations!

> *"Give often. Give generously. Give when you're debt-free."*

Be proud of yourself and what you've accomplished. Know that it was your will and determination that brought you through this. You have changed your life, and the lives of your family, in ways you probably don't even understand yet.

You did it, and we're proud of you!

Congratulations, and enjoy your new debt-free life!

GIVE THE GIFT OF FINANCIAL LITERACY

Now, it's time to give the gift of debt freedom to somebody else. Change somebody's life. Share this book with them. Share the tools you've used to seize control of your life, and help them find the peace that comes with being debt-free as well.

Give this book as a gift, maybe as a birthday present to a friend or as a graduation gift to your niece. Perhaps you go to church with somebody who is struggling, or you're in a club with somebody who needs help.

- Share it with them.

- Encourage them.

- Lead by example, and share your story as well.

Give the gift of financial literacy so others can zero down their debt and live life on their own terms. You know it's possible. Give them the courage, faith, and the tools to make it happen for them, too. On behalf of your friends, we thank you in advance.

ACTION ITEMS

Complete your emergency fund. Make sure that it is fully stocked with three to six months' worth of expenses.

Resume saving for retirement and your other savings goals. Start by saving 10% to 15% of your income in a work-sponsored retirement account. Once you've resumed retirement savings, consider saving for other goals, like college.

Use the money you've freed up to pay off your mortgage early. Make extra payments toward your mortgage, and knock out the last of your debt.

Enjoy living debt-free. Save for what you want. Give as generously as you can. Congratulations! You've earned it!

Give this book to a friend or family member. Share the tools you've used to become debt-free. Spread the love, the knowledge, and the wealth. There's enough for everybody to go around!

NOTES

NOTES

_____

_____

_____

_____

_____

_____

_____

_____

_____

_____

_____

_____

NOTES

NOTES

_____

_____

_____

_____

_____

_____

_____

_____

_____

_____

_____

MONTHLY EXPENSE REGISTER

EXPENSES	AMOUNT

MONTHLY SPENDING BY CATEGORY

EXPENSE CATEGORIES	TOTAL SPENT

AUTHORS' BIO

Holly Porter Johnson is an award-winning writer who focuses on frugality, budgeting, and credit as the cornerstones of her career. Greg Johnson is an entrepreneur who turned his love of budgeting and digital media into an online empire. Together, the power couple blogs about money at ClubThrifty.com, travels the world, and enjoys the good life with their two kids.